Growing Up
YORUBA

A Teen Guide Book
for Practicing
the Yoruba Lucumi Tradition

Kemba Mchawi

kembafilm@gmail.com

ISBN-10: 0615708749
EAN-13: 9780615708744

Remembrance

Ketema and Italo
We stop still. We hear you.
We live on today.
Stay

James Cooley (Iyawo Oshun Yemi) and Richard Franklin Jones, Sr.
James Mae Scarborough
Samuel C. Walker
Susie Walker
Jimmy Lillian Jones
Clifton Johnson
Nina Johnson
Ella Scarborough
Wilbur Chestnutt
Sudie Scarborough
Ara Scarborough
Fannie Scarborough
Alveda Suza Hill
Joyce Walker
Booker T. Walker
Phyllis Holmes
Marie Holmes

To the Ibae Elders who were in my ile or close to my heart
Omi Loke---Raymond Taylor
Okanturun – Richard Jordan
Olamide – Mary Curry
Shango Fo Shalade - Jean Purnell
Adeshola – Irene Blackwell
Omidina – Carol Ann Robinson
Iyawo Oshun Yemi – James Cooley
Adeleti – Wambui Smith
Omi Toki – Alfred Davis
OruOba – Mary Robinson
Ifa Alafia – Renaud Simmons
Alabumi – Jose Cheo Sardinas
Equin Leti –Rueben Rubio
Omi Laye - Carrie Lamont
Aya Ilu - Chief Bey
Ogunrelekun - Barbara Bey
Shangtosin – Genevieve Duncan
Oshun Aina - Pearl White
Olude - Dottie Holiday Martinez
Ibae Ibae Tonu

DEDICATION

Assata
Itala
Athena
Tiara
Masani
Folasade
Kamira
Kaleah

May you grow in the ways of our tradition

TABLE OF CONTENTS

FOREWORD

For some of us it was a matter of choice, but for others of us it was not. Religion has always had a way of forcing itself on populations that are certain that their faith is based on the reality that there is a Supreme Being and that the way of their kinfolk is the truest path to Him (or Her or It). Communal worship being the centerpiece of many cultures can be intimidating. But since everything else in successful societies appears to be organized that can be a good thing. Yet, considering today's definition of human, and particularly children's rights, there are often questions.

I was raised as a Christian, and when Christianity seemed to fail me I became secretly irreligious, but not unGodly. I saw religion as a weapon used against my race and the barrier that prevented Black people from effectively rallying to a common cause. However, believing very much in, and even loving God, I needed a reference and when I stumbled on the traditional religious format of Nigeria's Yoruba people, I had found gold. Here was an easy *choice*. It was a religion that centuries ago had been forbidden by slave owners to our ancestors who were forced to become Christians. So there was an automatic *cause*. And then It was the most poetically beautiful expression of the nature of creation and existence that I had ever seen or heard…and that was reason enough to study it and see it as sacred. And on top of all of that, It was African…and that was all I needed to dive in head first. It was my choice. I even became a priest.

But don't get me wrong, I was not alone or even a pioneer in this quest or this need. Among those who preceded me were my Godmother, my teacher and mentor, and it was she who some will say actually began the tradition of African American Ocha families, that is the raising of African American children who knew no other religion than Yoruba. Later, as priests with our own Orisha family, I and my wife Stephanie had a model to help instruct our own flock of parents who to our amazement and joy would raise their children in a tradition that in reality we were still trying to figure out. But still, despite our faith, we worried. Because we found fulfillment in making sacrifice to the Orisha, would children, growing up in an ethos that would see our practices as unorthodox, also share the love we had for worshipping in a format revealed by God to our ancestors centuries ago? How would they explain our non Christian practices to their friends? Would they be ridiculed for wearing white to school? What if they became overly-moved by the Orisha while in their classrooms? Yes, we sympathized and we worried.

Oddly though, our concerns were chiefly in our minds. At least that is what most of us have come to think because out of what must be hundreds, perhaps by now thousands, of Ocha children, grandchildren and great grandchildren all over America, indications are that very few have drifted away from our practices and reverted to Christianity or Islam or other options. In fact, nearly all of them are fully initiated Orisha priests, or aspire to be. How and why was this success rate achieved? Well, perhaps this book by Kemba Mchawi, the daughter of two pioneers in the spread of our religion (and now an Ocha parent herself) will give us some insight as to why and how Yoruba traditional religion became so meaningful to those who did not have a choice...those who, like her, grew up Yoruba!

Babalorisa Lloyd Weaver
Lagos, December 2012

PREFACE

So the problem with writing this book was finding the right voice to represent me. I can be so many people at so many times. Not in a Sybil multiple-personality type way; more like in a Dubois double-consciousness mode of functioning. You know, like being Black in America and having to walk in so many worlds. Try being a Black woman priest of Yemonja who grew up in a large communal Black Nationalist organization while simultaneously living in a home predominated by African religious practices while living in the hood in Bedford-Stuyvesant in a quasi-middle class family and trying to be a normal Brooklyn kid all at the same time. When I just *think* of all of this segueing into my later roles as college student, educator, mother, godmother, mother again, wife and lover, really like, what the freak...? You see each of these roles has a voice and a variation of purpose. So trying to figure out which "person" should write this book was my biggest challenge. At times I just walked away from it, returned, put it down again, but always, over and over again, I came back to it. So finally, finally, here we have it.... *Growing up Yoruba*. A user's guide for young people embarking in an experience that I have been a part of for most of my life. Thus I decided to go with the Kemba keeping and kicking it real voice.

This book is about the Yoruba-Lucumi religion from my perspective. It's intended to be my contribution to what is already a vast and growing body of literature on this subject. At any rate, my real hope is that for some of you it will fill a gap, spare you some pain, tell you when to laugh and help you to enjoy the benefits of what I feel is the most wonderful religion in the world! My prayer and my intention is to shed some light, from my perspective, on an authentically African way of seeing life while helping young people to still be themselves while applying an ancient and beautiful philosophy to a modern, ever changing and increasingly crazy world. This isn't as easy as it sounds because, let's admit it, our religion is different. It not Eastern and it is not Western. It is a God worshipping religion whose format and whose values and practices are African. Our practices are seen as odd and despite the ever diversifying religious environment of North America, as practitioners we stand out as peculiar. Finally, while *Growing Up Yoruba* is intentionally addressed to young people who are already coming up in this religion, I hope that others will learn something from it, as well.

As a matter of style, what you are about to read is a sharing of stories from my personal experience, all the while infusing what continues to be the Kembaesque approach to verve.

One more thing before we get started and to set the tone. You have to understand that African American practice of the Yoruba religion evolved from the experience of Cubans and is fundamentally the same. However as our numbers grew the fact that we spoke English instead of Spanish and aspired to enhance our Africaness rather than Latin led to variations in our ceremonial and ritual language. Even though I'm sure that you already know several terms that are peculiar to Yoruba religious practice many of these will still be further explained as we go along. However, before we go too far I want to mention two that for me may be the most important. Where Spanish speaking worshippers will address their elders as Madrina or Padrino, in most African American groups the terms (really titles) *Mama* and *Baba* always precede the names of adults when addressing or referring to ones elders. It is a traditional demonstration of respect that we are simply more comfortable with. Further, and this is still on the subject of respect, the real ritual language of our religion is Yoruba and all ceremonies and prayers begin with a formal remembrance of our deceased elders. You will notice that throughout this book the Yoruba word *ibae* precedes or antecedes the name of our *ultimate* elders, those who have preceded us to another realm. I am speaking of anyone who is deceased even if they were younger than you when they died. (Anyone who has completed his or her life on earth before you is now our elder).

You will love some of this book, though you may find some of it strange, maybe even offensive. You will discover some interesting angles on a lot of things, or you may disagree with other stuff. Hopefully, as you grow in the religion you will use this book not only as a learning tool, but ultimately as a *teaching* tool. OK, enough said. Let's get on with it.

INTRODUCTION

One thing I have noticed is that every book on Yoruba anything starts with "The Yoruba people of South West Nigeria were a large and accomplished people whose accomplishments in art and warfare", etc etc. So why would I start this way too? Well, because that's the African way; we always look at the past to understand our present position. When you acknowledge the past, you get all of the spiritual forces aligned and on your side. In fact, you may have noticed I started this book giving remembrance to my deceased ancestors and religious family. Well here is some Yoruba history.

The term *Yoruba* technically refers to the common language and culture of several large and ancient ethnic nations who for hundreds of years have lived and flourished in the southwestern region of Nigeria. Under the contentious suzerainty of the powerful Alaafin (or King) of Oyo, these kingdoms are referred to historically and collectively as the Oyo Empire. Now what this means is that if these kings didn't pay taxes to the Alaafin or send soldiers to fight in his army, he would kick their butt. OK, back to history. Highly accomplished as statesmen and artisans, merchants and intellectuals, the Oyo were both respected and feared far and near as all conquering warriors and empire builders. At its height, this decidedly old world empire was in many ways comparable to Rome or Carthage. Whereas Oyo exercised political suzerainty over kingdoms that spread from the Sahara Desert in the north to the Atlantic

Ocean in the south, and from Benin in the east to ancient Dahomey in the west (you should get a map), it even included the sacred city of Ile Ife, the revered spiritual capital believed to be the wellspring of the entire race and the source of its poetic and rich religious philosophy. In fact, Yoruba religious beliefs hold that on God's command, Ile Ife is the place where land first appeared above the sea spreading far and wide to cover much of this planet. According to Yoruba oral religious scripture, Ile Ife later became the cradle of mankind.

But moving closer to modern history, by the 19th century, a determined Islamic jihad from the north coupled with internecine disputes over power and control of the deteriorating Oyo Empire led to chaos. Everywhere refugees from the constant warfare wandered the vast area. Every ethnic nation had more captives than could safely be contained. At the same time, European desperation to capitalize on illegal claims to American territory found a convenient solution to their manpower problems as Africans readily traded hundreds of thousands of war captives for arms. Thus, alongside over ten million Africans who found themselves on the high seas bound as slaves for the so-called "new world" to work on farms and plantations, millions of Yoruba speaking slaves were dispersed throughout North, Central and South America. The highest concentrations were in Brazil, Trinidad, Puerto Rico and Cuba. According to Brandon in *Santeria from Africa to the New World: The Dead Sell Memories,* over 350,000 enslaved Africans from Yoruba nations were brought to Cuba alone. Most arrived in the Spanish controlled island just before the abolition of Cuban slavery in 1886. Conversations with the noted Yoruba anthropologist/historian Baba John Mason revealed that Africans were still being brought into Cuba as slaves as late as 1900 and that many of the formerly enslaved Yoruba were actually freed before the last captives reached Cuban soil.

Yet in the centuries before that, long hours of labor in the mountainous cane fields of the Caribbean islands under the punishing lash of slave drivers, had taken a cruel toll on the African captives. However, for many, the banning of African religion under the threat of death was the most dispiriting aspect of their captivity and, as years passed, many in fact did die for refusing to forsake the religion of their fathers. However, while we remember with reverence the true martyrs of our religion, history has it that by the latter half of the 19th century, many African farmers and hunters, travelers and especially warriors knew well the risk of being taken to a far place never to see their homeland again. Wisely, many carried relics and sacred items with them wherever they went. And sure enough, African religion, sewn into the pockets of unfortunate, but nevertheless clever priests now chained together in the bowels of ships, or even ingested to be secretly excreted in the land to which they were taken, endured and survived the Middle Passage. In other words, many slaves arrived literally 'with a trick up their sleeves.'

However, this African religion is far deeper than even its most sacred relics. Even more important were the critical and detailed *memories* of essential ancient practices that were carried in the *sacred heads* of the Orisha priests. And so, sealed in the seams of their tattered clothing or occasionally swallowed to be excreted and buried whenever they saw land again, but most importantly embedded by sacred ritual in the consecrated heads of very special people, a religion survived.

End of story? No. *Beginning* of story.

It was on arrival in the new world that Yoruba slave/priests and their followers faced the supposed *illegality* of what had been done to them. Clearly survival was still a question. Unwittingly however, the Europeans provided the means for survival in their own religious iconography. Thousands of enslaved Africans in places like Brazil and Cuba were able to mask their continued veneration of Orisha (Yoruba deities) above ground by pretending to worship Catholic saints. Over the course of two hundred years, the practice of ancestor and Orisha worship seemingly blended by syncretization with Catholic and other African cultures, evolved into what many African-Americans and Spanish-Americans today refer to as the Yoruba or Yoruba-Lucumi religion. (Though their language was generally banned, those who came from Yoruba speaking tribes generally greeted one another with the word 'Olukunmi', which means 'my friend.' For this reason, others began to refer to them as 'Lucumi.') Because of the predominance of Catholic images (mostly saints) in what were really Orisha shrines, in Spanish-speaking countries such as Cuba, Puerto Rico, and Mexico, the religion in its disguised form became known as Santeria (the worship of saints). In Brazil it is called Candomble; in Trinidad it is known as Shango.

Like I said, this little story has been told over and over in the prefaces of so many books dealing with Yoruba history, art, religion and culture. But it is retold here once more to imbue a sense of reverence or respect for those African heroes and heroines who preserved it with their very lives and thought up ways to pass to us an intact ritual (if you can forgive the changes in cosmetics) that was given by God to African people further back than anyone can remember. It is also recognition of the extraordinary privilege and responsibility we now have to those who risked their lives to preserve it even as slaves. Having said so much about the origins of the religion we now practice, and since, as you will soon see, most African Americans have changed the cosmetics from Spanish/Catholic back to African, for the purpose of this book, and with gratitude and respect to the Cuban Lucumi who so faithfully preserved this cherished tradition, I will proudly refer to our subject simply as the Yoruba religion.

The involvement of African-Americans in the Yoruba religion now spans over six decades. In 1959, two African-American pioneers, Baba

Christopher Oliana, ibae (Oba ilu mi), and Nana Oseijeman Adefunmi, ibae (Efuntola), traveled from the United States to Cuba to become initiated as priests of Aganju and Obatala. Baba Oseijeman, a colorful, charismatic genius, established The Yoruba Temple in Harlem, and later The Oyotunji Village in South Carolina. He was amazingly adept at Yoruba language, dress, dance and drumming in the 1960s, and in flowing robes, he led his followers singing and chanting through the streets of Harlem attracting hundreds of African Americans anxious to learn all they could about African culture and religion.

In 1963, Madrina Margie Quinones ibae (Shango Gumi) became the first African-American woman to be initiated here in the United States. As the godmother of my godfather, Baba Lloyd, Madrina Margie was an important person in my Ile (community of worshippers, also referred to as 'house'). She was also *ojubona*, (second godparent) to my mother, Mama Oseye and to one of my mother's godsister's, Mama Robinson, ibae (Obatala Priest). Madrina Margie's godmother, Madrina Leonore Dome, ibae (Omi Duro) was Cuban. Madrina Leonore, like many Cubans, had migrated to the United States after Fidel Castro overthrew the Fulgencio Batista led Cuban government. And, like scores of Cubans of African cultural descent, brought with her, carefully kept Yoruba religious practices. The timing was perfect. It coincided with a sociopolitical African-centered movement that was already taking place here in the United States. It was the time of the push for civil rights from which the Black Power, and Black Pride movements eventually evolved. It was the time when we changed from being "Negroes" to African Americans. And I should mention here that it was in the sixties that many African nations, including Nigeria, emerged from their independence struggles as proud independent nations and many African Americans looked to Africa for inspiration and identification.

Thus, the appearance of Baba Oseijeman, Baba Chris Oliana, Madrina Margie Quinones and Madrina Leonore Dome was auspicious. And I should also mention that other Latinos initiated African Americans as well, most notably Madrina Sunta Serrano, ibae (Osaunko) a Puerto Rican Obatala Priestess whose dozens of African American godchildren are a like a sister house to my own.

So it was in the sixties that African Americans ubiquitously embraced African names, foods, and hairstyles in many parts of the United States. African music, long a big part of twentieth century American culture influencing ragtime, jazz, blues, rock and roll and rhythm & blues, was now becoming a mainstay in pop culture. In New York City, and also in Miami where Latin music had been popular even in the forties and fifties, Cuban music encompassed the use of African drums and instruments, rhythmic dancing, and African styles of singing using call and response became the "thing."

With the historical camaraderie between Latinos that included Cubans, Puerto Ricans, Dominicans, Panamanians, etc. and African Americans, an appreciation of the African religious values that the Latinos had preserved, has led to hundreds of African-Americans making repeated journeys to Cuba in search of further religious edification.

But what is most amazing is the phenomena of who knows how many hundreds of African Americans who have been initiated right here in America. There have been over one hundred initiations in my Ocha house alone. Many of the priests in my Ocha house have become godparents, teachers, and artisans on the religion themselves. And even without these distinguishing factors, many have learned the secrets and beauty of this religion through years of guided instruction and participation. (See appendix included). By the way, the term "Ocha" is the Latin pronunciation of Orisha and is used interchangeably even by African Americans. As I was saying, African-American priests of

Orisha are now spread throughout the United States, with significant numbers living in New York, California, and Florida, as well as Houston, Baltimore, Washington, DC, Chicago, Detroit, and so forth. Our religious practices have forged relationships among Cubans, Puerto Ricans, Brazilians, Nigerians, and other nationalities of the African diaspora. Although most of us were not born in Africa, and most may not even be sure that our ancestral lineage is traceable to the Yoruba people, we still call ourselves Yoruba because of our ardent practice of Yoruba religious traditions.

But even though someone said that the "past is prologue," that is not the real concern here. Our concern is that we are the prologue. Our world is very different from that in which our parents pioneered the re-inclusion of African religion in the spiritual mix of African American religious practices. Though their historical and insightful initiatives will always be honored, the world of today is clearly different with different concerns. So it must be asked, for young African Americans growing up in Yoruba households, what is the real relevance of our religion to the social, cultural and political challenges that we face today? While racism is still predominant in America, in many ways the civil rights movement is now over, with one of the outcomes being the firmness of our identity as a people of African descent. But what about this Yoruba religion? Despite the overwhelmingly Judeo-Christian environment that we live in, what keeps people struggling to incorporate these alien values in their daily lives? Hopefully this book will provide some answers to these questions through my eyes as I grew up Yoruba.

Chapter I
Mi Beginning

My mother grew up in the church. And so did her mother and my great-grandmother as well. But that pathway was to end for me because when I was seven years old my mother joined the Yoruba religion, I mean body and soul. She came upon it easily. Had her third baby, and there it was. Mom never looked back. It's interesting how the religion found her, when for many years she had searched for the right religious practice for her life. Along the road, she had been Baptist, Seventh-day Adventist, Pentecostal, Methodist, Catholic, and had even dabbled in the study of Islam. None of them worked for her. But this Yoruba thing did. From the beginning she felt a connection, a simple drawing to it like no other.

Funny, it's not like we really had a religion before Mom became Yoruba; however, I do recollect that my brother and I occasionally went to church with my grandparents. Plus, I do know we were christened as babies; my great-great aunt Ella was my first godmother. But at home with my mother I don't remember religion before becoming Yoruba. What I do remember is being raised in an African oriented semi-communal atmosphere that my whole family belonged to called "The East". They encouraged a total African lifestyle and value system; I even attended a private school called Uhuru Sasa Shule (Swahili for Freedom Now School). It was kind of cool as far as I was concerned. The organization was headed by Brother Jitu Weusi, ibae, a long time educator, activist and pan-Africanist leader. There, they changed my name from Vikki-Leigh to Kemba, and my older brother's name from Richard to Ketema. We were told that we needed African names to represent who we were in the world, rather than our previous "slave" names. Kemba means "faithful one," and Ketema means "king of the valley."

Our school life was very different from others in our neighborhood with longer school days and African styled uniforms; we learned Swahili, and every subject we learned had something to do with Africa. Mom didn't know it then, and my brother and I certainly didn't either, but this had to have been a divine precursor to prepare us for what was to come. So I wasn't really surprised a few years later when our mother wanted us to join this African religion.

My mom, Oseye Mchawi during a special chieftaincy ceremony, Ibadan, Nigeria 1990. She already had 16 years of Obatala at this time.

Baba – Basir Mchawi longtime educator and community activist.

In June of 1974, when I was seven, my mother gave birth to her second daughter. We were not told her name because my mother and Baba, informed us that there would be a naming ceremony. Early one Sunday morning, when my little sister was about a week old, everyone from The East community gathered in our small Herkimer Street apartment in Brooklyn to witness the naming ceremony of my baby sister. A man and his wife, Baba Lloyd and Mama Stephanie, both priests in the Yoruba religion, performed the ceremony. They would later become our family's godparents. Food was arranged on the floor in the kitchen for our ancestors, and the priest prayed, chanted, and performed a sacrifice over the makeshift shrine on the floor. It was odd. Even at my African school, I had not seen anything like this. It was my earliest memory of giving offerings to my ancestors.

From there everyone followed the two priests into the living room. Baba Lloyd asked my parents to whisper the baby's name into the ear of the baby's godfather. He then asked the godfather to announce the baby's name to the community, which he proceeded to do. In the most grandest of fashion, the godfather told all of us who awaited the dramatic moment that the baby's name was Zuwena Isoke. He told us the name means "a good, satisfying gift from God." At that point, Baba Lloyd took the baby from her godfather and held the baby before him with his arms stretched high above his head to present her to Olofi/God. He told her there was nothing greater than herself but God. It was just like a scene in the movies *Roots*, except this was before *Roots* had aired.

When that was over, people sat on chairs, bean cushions, and the floor with their legs folded or spread out before them. Baba Lloyd took off his shoes and sat on an *estera*, (a straw, beach-style mat used for saluting, or sitting an Orisha on). My baby sister's godfather also took off his shoes and sat facing the priest. The godfather held the baby for the entire ceremony. Baba Lloyd passed around plates with different

5

ingredients like salt, sugar, and palm oil, water honey, gin etc. Each item was symbolic of a value or experience to be encountered in life; a prayerful preview of things to come in order to prepare baby Zuwena for the future. Her godfather put a little of each item in her mouth, and the rest of us had to taste each item as well.

Then there was a reading, a sort of recitation from the Yoruba scripture, telling everyone some of what of the new baby was called to do in life. Other people also spoke and said nice things and offered their blessings. Afterward, everyone got up, and the priest led us in a song; we each had to dance with the baby and whisper a message in her ear. Finally, finally we were able to eat; there was a lot of food, which reminded me of pictures I had seen in school of feasts in African villages.

My godfather, Baba Lloyd Weaver and Nana Oseijeman Adefunmi

Although my mother had just met Baba Lloyd and Mama Stephanie that day through Baba, she was enthralled by the experience. We all could see that a sense of longing to know more about this religion had begun. Shortly afterwards, she scheduled her own reading with Baba Lloyd and was told that the Orisha (Yoruba deities) were calling for her, and that she needed to be initiated in the tradition. This isn't something

7

that happens to everyone. Some people get readings that are just like consultations; they get the advice and are off about the business of their life. Then there are others who Orisha call to faithfully include this religion as a part of their lives. So, two years later, in 1976, after numerous fundraisers including fish fries, street corner baby clothing sales, and African Street Festival crab sales, my mother was initiated into the tradition as a priest of Obatala. It was a huge occasion. I was nine at the time, but I remember all the people and the busyness of it all. My mother was initiated with another woman, Mama Irene, ibae, who was initiated as a priest of Aganju. Later, I'll tell you a little about Obatala and Aganju. Anyway, prior to this big event, I used to wonder when my mother was going to give up all this weird religious stuff. Ha! It wasn't to happen. During the seven days my mom spent on the specially built throne, my brother and I received *ilekes*, (special beads that represent your own connection to the Orisha). Receiving your *ilekes* is the first step in being initiated in the religion. So this is how, at nine years old, I made my first committed step in being a part of the Yoruba religion. At that time, I really didn't know what I was doing, but it was interesting and has been ever since.

THE EARLY YEARS

THERE WERE TWO THINGS THAT BOTHERED ME the most about my mother's new religion. First, our Bed-Stuy Brooklyn brownstone became Grand Central station. Everybody came to our house, whether they had a toothache, paranoia-schizophrenia or the plain old blues. My mother had something like an unspoken open-door policy and the whole of Brooklyn knew it. A lot of them were cool people. But cool or not, all of her godchildren knew they could just come by our house for anything at anytime. They wouldn't even knock on the door. They just entered at will. To my mother's dismay, I was always hollering out at one or the other of them to freakin' knock before they entered, you know, show some respect. There were other people who lived in the house besides my mother.

At this point, my sibling pool had increased to include one more sister, Mandisa, and another brother, Italo. My brother, Ketema and I were largely responsible for helping to take care of them. I also now had a stepsister, Abena, four years my junior; she didn't live with us, but I liked when she came over because she always wanted to play with my hair.

Anyway, the second thing that set me off was when some of my mother's godchildren would come to the house and try to boss me around. That just wasn't happening, not with this girl. Big arguments ensued. I couldn't believe her godchildren could have the balls to come into my house and tell me to clean up the living room or fold the clothes or stay out of the kitchen. Stay out the kitchen? Stay out of the kitchen? Kiss my ass! This was *my* house, and that was a battle they were definitely not going to win. Well, unless my mother was within ear or eyesight. It seemed like in every instance she would side with them, and I, reluctantly, with pouted lips and much attitude, had to comply with their wishes. Those people!

Thinking about that lot of people as a whole, I have to say I hated them. I mean, I really did. They had too many rights in our house. And they were always there. Till this day, I think that is why there are times when I just love being in my own home alone. But when I think of each of them on an individual level, I know I really loved most of them. They were smart and talented and taught me a lot. Honestly good people, really family like, and so even though I had plenty of angry moments,

I'd be lying low like a snake if I didn't say it was mostly good times in the house with all the laughing, gossiping, and crazy stories.

Me (big-eyes) with my siblings Mandisa, Ketema, Zuwena, and Italo.

When I think about some of my typical weekends growing up with a mother who was totally involved in the religion, it would look like this: It's Saturday afternoon. All I can think about is going to the mall with my friends. The new Stan Smith Adidas are going on sale, and I would love to use my saved up fifteen dollars along with the extra forty bucks I planned on bumming off my grandparents to get a new pair. I'd start off with something like "Hola, Mommy, what's going on?" followed up with "So, what are we doing today?"

In seconds, I wish I could take back the rhetorical question because, like I said, I already had my own agenda, but my mother answers, "Oh, we're going to a *bembe* today" (A bembe is a kind of festival for the Orisha with drumming and dancing and food and everybody in the fast growing Orisha world).

"A bembe? Mommy, please not another bembe! We just went to one last Saturday. Do I have to go?"

"Yep," she replies easily yet firmly, dismissing any thoughts I had of doing something else.

OK, so here I am at the *bembe.* No new sneakers today. Store closed tomorrow. Forget about asking to go during the school week. Guess I'd better try again next week. But if I know my Mom, next week, there will be something else. And it's not like I don't like the *bembes*, it's just that it isn't what my friends are doing. Plus, it isn't as if I am going to meet any new people at the bembes, like I would at the mall, where I could meet some fine homeboys or just hang out with my crew.

It definitely was not easy growing up in a religion that was different from the norm in society. No matter how many things I had in common with my friends, I knew there was a line that separated me from them.

I lived a different life. I lived an experience that they would never understand. There weren't any green bananas hanging over their doors.

But with all of the spiritual activity around me, I had different feelings and a different sense of awareness. And somewhere along the way, I even started to like it, and to even rely on it. You know, difference is the spice of life. And there is nothing wrong with having a unique flavor.

So the question for me became this: how do I function in this world—all Americanized, with my Yorubacized life—and still remain cool? Kicking down the cobblestone streets of life, I discovered it was all about balance. That's right, **B** to the **A** to the **L** to the **A** to the **N** to the **C** to the **E**. So when the "aha" moment came; it sailed into a confused mind of whys, how comes, and sighs, and broke open wide to expose a clear beauty like sunrays canvassing the ocean. Yes, "aha": if I could figure out how to incorporate this religion into my life—and not just through parental force but because I really wanted to be down with the program—and somehow still do me, I could have the best of both worlds.

Plus, I did have some friends who were also part of the religion. Two of my closest friends parents were initiated in the religion. There was Wacheera. She is my godfather's first daughter, and was initiated by my godmother. Then there was Yvette. Her mother, Mama Ayo is my god-aunt in the religion (she is my godmother's godsister). Because of her mother's deep knowledge and study on the Yoruba tradition, Yvette knew back then more about the religion than most of us young folks. Yvette and I have remained friends throughout the years, and we still consider ourselves cousins. Along with them, I shared my youth in the Yoruba religion with my other close friend-cousin. That was Fahja. In those days, she and I were inseparable, going to many of the ceremonies, and bembes together. Her mother, Brenda, ibae was part of the religion, but she never went through the ceremony to become fully initiated as a priest. Today, Fahja is a devout Christian, but our friendship remains intact. Joe-T was also a friend of mine growing up, although our first meeting wasn't that great. I was sporting a short afro hair cut, and he thought I was a boy. He had the nerve to ask my brother Ketema, "who's that little boy over there?' Till this day, we sometimes laugh about that. Joe-T is the son of Madrina Margie, ibae, and brother to three older siblings who were also initiated priests: David, ibae (an Obatala priest), Kittie (a Yemonja priest), and Keke (an Oshun priest). Joe-T made Ocha in his teens, a few years behind his best friend Jackie. My mom made Jackie's Ocha when he was very young, and my godfather made Joe-T, so basically I was around them a lot and we were all pretty close back then.

When I think about it, there were actually a number of other people around my age that I hung out with, like Earl, Ava (an Obatala priest), Sade, Dara, Maisha, Frankie (a Shango priest), and Juwandi (an Oshun priest). Their families were also heavily involved in the religion.

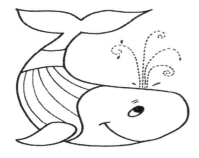

Hey, perhaps "this is the best of all possible worlds," as Voltaire's Candide said so often. And this was what I was beginning to see. When I began to create a sense of balance in my life, all things became clear. I was able to navigate between being the fly and popular girl I was while also being devoted to my religious spiritual life. I was able to hang out at the basketball tournaments on West Fourth Street in the city with Fahja, Yvette, and my other best friend cousin Yolanda who was originally from Brooklyn but spent her teen years growing up in Rochdale Village in Queens. Being tight with Yolanda, I would spend many weekends making the two-train-and-a-bus trek out to her home where she lived with her grandparents, her brother Ronald, and Aunt Vanessa. Yolanda's mother, Impress Ima, a true queen Rastafarian woman lived in Harlem at that time, so we got our share of hanging out in the city with her, as well.

But anyway, if I wasn't chillin' in Manhattan or Queens, I'd be right in Brooklyn checking out the b-ballers at The Soul in the Hole tournaments at PS 44 Park on Monroe Street. It was always good catching up with any one of my fly-ass Bed-Stuy friends like Nick, Squirt, Eighty-Eight, Warren, Fruquan, Sydney, Cynthia, Janeece, or Louise, and then later in the evening, head back home to help my mother and her army of godchildren with one of the usual weekend ceremonies. Changed up clothes; put on my whites, tied up my head, re-kissed my illekes, and was ready to work. Sometimes it called for taking a quick spiritual bath. All of it, no problem. Just a part of me.

Eventually being Yoruba became more than just a religion. It was what I did. In time, it became my way of living life.

Asha and me on a typical Brooklyn day. Asha's family is part of The East. Several of her relatives are Yoruba practitioners.

CHAPTER II

MI SPIRITS

During one of my earliest readings, I was told that I needed to develop spiritually. My godmother told me I needed to set up an *obobera*, (also called boveda) which is a table dedicated to praying to the ancestors that contains offerings, to give light and prayer to my ancestors, spiritual guides and protectors. She told me that I needed to sit at my obobera and pray and meditate. OK.

SO WHAT DOES IT MEAN TO DEVELOP SPIRITUALLY?

THE WAY THAT THE YORUBA SEE IT (and a lot of other folks for that matter), we are all spiritual beings. We come into the world as spirits with bodies. As we grow and move in the world, there are all these other spirits around us. Some of the spirits are deceased members of our family. They may be family members you actually knew or family members that were deceased before you were born but have watched over you and made sure that you are safe in the world: a deceased parent, sibling, grandparent or great grandparent, or aunt or uncle. Really, any blood family member.

However, not all, maybe not even most of the spirits around you are your folks. These other spirits can also be your spiritual guides and protectors. They are around to guide you in the right direction in life. They are also there to help you and keep you out of harms' way. In helping you let's just say they get credit for their own evolution. But the other reason that they are around you is so that you can help them..mostly by praying for their upliftment, development and progress.

I remember a time back when a fight broke out on my block and all of my friends, including me, ran to see the throw down. I loved a good fight, despite the fact that my parents had told me over and over, "Don't run to trouble, run away." Well, when I got there, I could see hair getting pulled and faces getting slapped. Choice profanity was torpedoing everywhere. Oh, it was so good. I was pumped up from the excitement. But as I stood there in the midst of the madness, hopping up every few seconds to get a better view of the fight, I noticed a lot of pushing going on in the crowd. It didn't seem related to the fight—just really random. Something started tugging at me to walk away. *Yo, yo, get out of there, head back to the house.* I was hearing it but at the same time I didn't want to miss this shit, because now clothes were being ripped. The voice was still there, but I wasn't even trying to listen.

Now I can only think that my spiritual guide/protector must have kicked into turbo gear, because now the voice was screaming in my ear, really clouding my brain to the point of causing me slight physical pain; I couldn't even enjoy the fight anymore. Reluctantly,

I turned around and headed back to my house. Although I felt like I was missing something, the voice was subsiding, and I was starting to feel a little lighter. You know, more at ease, like somehow I knew I was doing the right thing.

Suddenly, as I approached the gate to the front yard of my house, I heard the first gunshot ring out. It was followed by a succession of pops. Everybody back at the scene, which thank goodness I had left already, was screaming and running like wildfire. I ran four steps and was in the house safely. My heart, liver, lungs, and blood were jumping out of my epidermis. It doesn't take a gypsy to see my fortune. I was so grateful that I didn't get caught up in that melee.

So, who was there to thank for saving me from the danger of that moment? Surely not my own nosey, thrill-seeking self! Maybe my parents; yeah, they deserved some credit, but remember, I had not listened to them when they forewarned me not to run to a fight in the first place. Perhaps, then, it was that spiritual guide watching over me. "The voice" as I called it. Not like the voice in an old Vincent Price and Boris Karloff movie (Google them), that kind of speaks to you from overhead. Nah, not like that. The voice is sort of within. It's familiar. It's something I have heard all my life. Sometimes softly. Sometimes very loudly, like in this case. I was thankful to my spiritual guide for warning me. But I was also thankful to myself, because I knew enough to listen.

And that is why I say that you have to do things for your guides and protectors as well…and the obobera is where you go to do it. The obobera? Right, that's where you go to pray for them and also get advice and, well, kind of hang out.

Anyhow, it's likely that you have these good spirits around you, but sometimes as you go through life you also pick up bad spirits on the road. You know just like there are good and bad people, there are good and bad spirits and they all fight to influence you according to their own character. The bad ones can lead you to do destructive things, or create harm for you. You will need to either get rid of these spirits (preferably) or help them to change. That's where prayer comes in. Bottom line is, it's important that you pay homage to your ancestors and spiritual guides.

SO IT'S TIME FOR YOU TO PUT TOGETHER A SPIRITUAL ALTAR

IT'S CALLED AN OBOBERA AND IT BECOMES the center-piece of your relationship with your spiritual guides and protectors. OK. Now we are going to set one up. When you start off, you generally need three clear glasses filled with fresh, clear water.

Your main glass is what most people in my group call the "God glass" because it's dedicated to God, and it is the biggest of the three.

Sometimes we use a medium sized fish bowl. The other two more ordinary glasses are equal in size. One is dedicated to your ancestors (those related to you by blood). The other glass is dedicated to your spiritual guides and protectors.

You want to put this altar on a table, shelf, or somewhere where you can go to sit and meditate. Some people put it up high, like on the refrigerator, but that can become awkward because you really won't spend enough time there. You need to cover your altar area with a white piece of cloth if the area isn't white already.

In the smaller glasses, you want to put a small white candle in each, and in the God glass you want to place a cross (you know, a crucifix) in the water. As you place each glass on the altar, you first need to lift it high and say, "I'm dedicating this glass to my ancestors" or "to my spiritual guides and protectors," or "to God." As time goes on, you may need to add additional glasses to your altar; these other glasses represent specific eguns (ancestors, spiritual guides, or spiritual protectors) or a group of people more specifically, like Native American guides (the spirits of the original people who lived in North America are all around us) or Congo guides. (Congos are a categorical reference to African guides that are not necessarily Yoruba).

My grandfather, James Cooley, Iyawo Oshun Yemi, ibae

LOOKS GOOD, BUT HOW WILL IT HELP ME?

ONCE YOU HAVE YOUR ALTAR IN PLACE, you're probably wondering, *OK, so now what do I do with it?* Along with using it as a place to say prayers, your spiritual altar designates a space to relax and meditate. Through meditation and relaxation you will become more attuned to your inner self—something we all have. That inner self is always battling to find peace, and to find strength, but most of the time we are so caught up in what's happening in our lives at the moment that we don't take the time to listen to it and honor it. You ever wake up some mornings and feel uncomfortable or unsettled, even though you had a full night's sleep? Or perhaps the sun isn't shining. It makes you feel sort of gloomy. You really don't want to go to school—you don't even want to get out of the bed. If you were to go and sit a few minutes in front of your obobera, say a few prayers and just soothe your inner self, it would help you to feel better and stronger about the day.

Being quiet, taking deep breaths, and focusing will help you to improve your entire outlook on life. Spiritual guru Deepak Chopra talks about going into a state of silence for a period of time. It could just be for thirty minutes, a few hours, or even some days. When you stop talking, you can calm and connect with your inner self. It is a great practice. I often incorporate this into my household routine with my teenage girls.

Ever been in a good mood, and then a friend calls you and unloads all his or her problems on you, and by the time you hang up you're feeling all funky and bluesy? Then it's time to *clean off*. Your obobera is an important place to go to "clean off." To clean off means to remove all the invisible negative murk that you have collected on your spirit self over a period of days, or even over one day. Sometimes you'll go into a place that will for no apparent reason dampen your spirits. You need to clean that off of you. I remember the instruction of my godsister Mama Joan on how to "clean off". She demonstrated how to pass your hands that have been dipped in specially prepared water over the top of your head and back of your neck then flick it away from you. Next, she moved on using her fingers to clean her temples, and her forehead, then again flicked the water away from her body. Lastly she dipped her hands in the water again, and cleaned downward from her neck to her toes, again flicking the water away from her body. Her hands acted as the invisible cloth, and the flicking it away, was like getting the spiritual murk away from you.

Many of us are spiritual sponges; we often pick up on people's negative energy, and it will attach to us like barnacles on the bottom of a ship. You would be amazed at how quickly negative energy can spread from one person to another person. Cleaning off at the obobera lightens things up. It makes you feel spiritually lighter and refreshed.

Now, about that special water. You can half fill a basin with ordinary tap water and add special ingredients to it. We often put it on the floor in front of the obobera. One of the main things you use to clean off at the *obobera* is something called Florida Water. You can also use other kinds of special water like rose water, Pompeii, *kologna*, Indian luck cologne, etc. You know, those sweet smelling waters you find in botanicas or spiritual stores. If you have none of that at the time, you can always clean off with toilet tissue, or just good ol' H_2O, as another godsister, Mama Mtam would so readily remind me.

Being spiritually unclean can stagnate your growth. The inner light that illuminates you will seem a little duller, and you won't be able to quite feel your best. When you don't feel good, it affects everything around you. Cleaning off regularly at your obobera will oftentimes alleviate depressive and hopeless feelings.

OH GEEZ, HOW TO PRAY

SAY IT AGAIN AND AGAIN: "REPETITION IS the mother of all learning." One of the first things you want to do is learn some prayers. Then say them again and again. *The Lord's Prayer* and the *Twenty-Third Psalm* are pretty good ones because they cover the basic tenets of what we are seeking, and they are direct prayers to God. Why Christian prayer? Well because your guides and protectors were Christian, that's why, and what you are doing is to and for them. Besides, It's easier for us to say the Christian prayers in this setting because one, they're in English, so we understand, and two, many of our ancestors recognize these prayers, having come up as Christians through the traumatic experiences of slavery and post-slavery. In other words, it's about understanding the real nature of the spirit world and being firm in the knowledge that spirits from our preceding four or five past generations will be the closest to us. Most of them were practicing Christians, and if we want to worship with and work with them we have to have that in mind. We have to begin by speaking the same language and singing the same songs they did.

Most spirits that are still within our reach are attracted to the things they dealt with during their previous incarnations. They carry the same tastes and attitudes and values. If they were peace loving when they were alive they are likely to be peace loving as spirits. If they were thieves when they were alive then they might be thieves now and encourage you to take what you want. I mean really. That's why we pray for them to evolve. But we meet them where they are and call them in a form and format that is familiar. So since most of our now deceased peeps were (and are) deep seated Christians, they respond most easily to Christian prayers.

In other words, our forefathers in Africa had their own special ceremonies in how they worshipped Egun, like the Egungun ceremony (*ceremony involving a masquerade dance celebration through the streets*), and their spirits responded to this because it was recognizable to what they (the spirits) had experienced when they were alive. However, our immediate ancestors did not live their lives in Africa, and would probably run for the hills if we came at them with some sort of masquerade venerating service. But if we came to them with some pretty smells, light a candle and start reciting the *Lord's Prayer* and sing *Swing Low Sweet Chariot*, we would more than likely become more in tune with those immediate spirits around us.

After you get familiar with some of your spiritual guides who love your voice when you sing *His Eye is On The Sparrow*, you can sit and have a discussion and maybe even reach a compromise on the format of your relationship. But it will take more than a minute. First, you have to give them some good old established respect. In other words a little "Our Father who art in Heaven..." will go a long way. First it's about establishing empathy and you can't do that by scaring them away. So it really is okay to set up your oboberas with your Bibles (yes Bibles) and your crucifixes and your water glasses and with real African wisdom. Actually, it's the most African thing you will ever do in your life.

So again, learn some prayers. Of course, there are plenty out there, or you really can create your own. The point here is to know a few basic prayers and keep reciting them at your altar, even if you have to read them. Eventually you'll remember them without looking. There are also books you can use to recite prayers, such as Allen Kardec's *Collection of Selected Prayers*. This book is used by millions of people around the world, and by using it yourself you will become part of a big support group whose prayers are recognized quickly in the spirit world. Like I said. "Repetition."

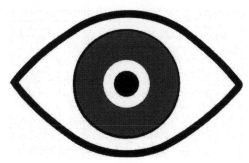

Praying will help to quiet your mind. When you can quiet your mind of all the million and one thoughts that flow through it, then you can relax and prepare to be in a meditative state to actually receive messages from your guides. Controlling your breathing is an important step when trying to meditate. You must train your breathing to be slower and drawn out longer. Try breathing in deeply through your nose, hold it for a few seconds, then exhale slowly through your mouth. Repeat this cycle several times, and you should feel yourself becoming more at ease. Ultimately, prayer will make you feel stronger, like **MC Hammer said: "That's why we pray, pray; we got to pray just to make it today."**

WHY SPIRITUALLY DEVELOP?

CONTRARY TO WHAT WE WANT TO BELIEVE, we really were not put on this earth to make a lot of money or to get fly gear, a big house, and a fat car. It's really not all about all that—that stuff is fringe. But we live in a world that forgets what life's emphasis should really be; instead we take the fringe and act like it's the main event. Negative. Not. You see it when there are people with loads of money who can buy whatever they want in the world, and yet they are still unhappy. Recognize that. I mean, what are they missing? Their external self—the one that reps for the world—is chilling and looking good. But truth be told they need to satisfy the inner self—the one that counts.

Developing spiritually puts you on the path to recognizing and identifying what your inner self needs. Some things are fundamental, but it ain't all the same for all folks because here is where *purpose* plays a part. John's inner self may be calling for him to express himself through paintings, while Kevin's inner self may be seeking for him to express and show divine purpose through writing. Sheila's inner self may be expressed through charity work or other philanthropic things. Whatever it is, it's bigger than just making money and achieving fame. This is not to say that you can't make money and that you shouldn't have nice things. Please do. Wait. Let me emphasize, I mean really, please, please do that. But you must make sure that you have balance. Balance is everything. Do a lil this, do a lil that. Have a lil this, have a lil that. Trust—balance is the key to getting right in the mind, body, and soul.

Now I think that by talking about spirits and spiritualism with Christian devices and references you have a practical feel for how and why it all works. So now let's put it back in the context of the Yoruba religion. To worship *Orisha* you must worship both *Egun* and *egun*. Same word in terms of spelling and both, in different ways, apply to the dead. But they are different. In a minute we will get into what an Orisha actually is and then we will explain the Orisha of the dead called Egun (Big E). Meanwhile, you have to know that the spirits that we have just described (you know your spirit guides and protectors) are called egun(little e) in Yoruba so when people talk about their or your eguns you know what they mean. Now if that's confusing just read it again and you'll get it.

So, anyway, **it is our duty to take care of our eguns just like it's their duty to take care of us.** It is a reciprocal relationship. The things on your *obobera* are the simple things that you are offering to your eguns. As times goes on, you may discover you need to add something else—a piece of family memorabilia, a doll or statue, or just about anything. Your eguns will tell you what they need.

One of the things that we do as a group to receive messages from our eguns and to give them our thoughts and wishes and prayers is to occasionally attend a ceremony sometimes called a "spiritual mass." That means a ceremonial prayer session that involves prayers for, to and with spirits. In other words, the spirits are called to participate in the prayer session. In the Latino communities they call it a *misa* or *misa blanca* or a *centro*. We often call it a "centro" as well. Anyway, at these settings mediums will get messages from spirits for different people. Many times messages can come through mediums while they are in a meditative state. On some occasions the medium may become possessed with a spirit and talk or behave differently. I'm using the word "mediums," but any of us can be a medium—we all have the ability; some of us are just more spiritually developed or attuned than others. All the prayers and spiritual songs, the white table, the smells from the items used to clean the space, all serve to create an atmosphere that is the catalyst for interaction with spirits. It signals to the spirit world that a group of people have assembled and prepared themselves for a spiritual session. And spirits come, oh boy do they come. *Centros* can swing from being calm to wildly exciting. Personally, I used to love the wild ones. And don't let somebody's egun come down talking slave talk. *"Oh my good Lordy, cotton needs a-picking sooo bad."* I would be tripping. It can be like a movie. But the messages that are conveyed were usually on point. Some of the stuff I used to learn about people's lives was unbelievable. Fortunately, my godmother told me, "You are not supposed to talk people's business to others that were not present at the *centro*." Mostly, I honored that.

Taking care of these altars can sometimes be tedious and a pain in the butt, but it's important to just get in the routine of doing these things. After a while, it will be normal to you, like getting dressed.

The best part is, it will really make you feel better and brighter about your day and your plans. Like I was saying, we have a give-and-take relationship with our eguns. Go to them and tell them what you want; ask for their help; ask for their advice. What egun wants and needs from us is a *connection*. Helping egun in their spiritual realm makes our earthly realm a little more hip, funky, and tolerable. And purposeful.

Part of the practice of keeping spiritually clean is to routinely commune with your eguns, relate to them and get them in order. The ultimate is to get them to understand your aspirations for accomplishment as a living person and for growth as a spiritual person. Like you, for most of them, their ultimate aspiration is to evolve. They need your prayers for that. As 21st century African Americans seeking to practice an African religion format for worshiping God, we have embarked on a journey that can be long and arduous because so many generations of Christians have characterized our lineage. But if the spirits of those who lived their entire lives as Christians can become even closer to us, if they can be convinced to step aside, and give us their blessings, the road to African spirituality, including the worship of Olofi through Orisha, can be the experience that fate has held in store for you since you were born. You can't just bypass your grandmother, and your great grandmother and your great great grandmother, and get on a plane to Africa and connect with somebody else's eguns. That is unless you have dealt with your own historical eguns first and you know that they willingly got on the plane with you. And remember, if you haven't done this it's never too late. But at some point, you have to respectfully and humbly deal with your genuine lineage and work your way back. It can be so enjoyable because it's real and you know where you stand each step of the way.

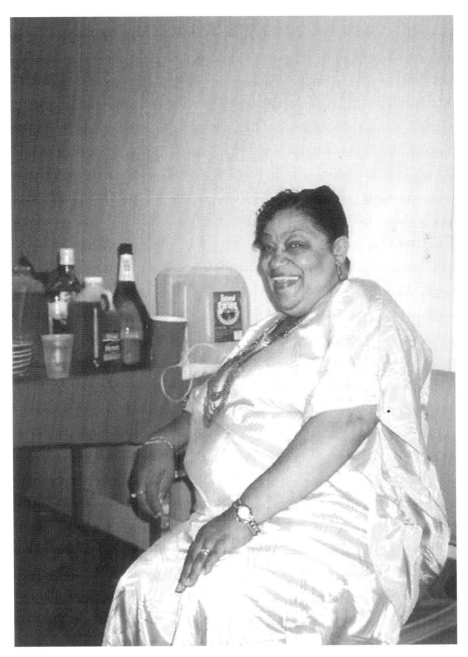

*Mama Dottie Holiday Martinez, ibae. Oshun priest – she was like a
mother to me and many others in Atlanta.*

SPIRITUAL SONGS TO SING AT A CENTRO
OR AT YOUR OBOBERA

This little light of mine
I'm going to let it shine
This little light of mine
I'm going to let it shine
This little light of mine
I'm going to let it shine
Let it shine, let it shine, let it shine
Harry Dixon Loes

Somebody prayed for me
They had me on their mind
They took the time to pray for me
I'm so glad they prayed
I'm so glad they prayed
I'm so glad they prayed for me
Dorothy Norwood and Melvin Darling

We are Soldiers in the Army
We have to fight although we have to die
We have to hold up the blood-stained banner
We have to hold it up until we die
Unknown

Gonna lay down my burdens
Down by the riverside—down by
Down by the riverside—down by
Down by the riverside—
Gonna lay down my burdens
Down by the riverside
I ain't gonna study war no more
Plantation Melodies, 1918

Also, some of us like to include the spirituals used by slaves to secretly celebrate the fact that they were Africans and express their longing to return, or sometimes to encourage rebellions or celebrate victories over white slave owners. Such songs included:

Go down Moses,
Way down to Egypt land
Tell Ol Pharaoh
To Let my people Go
Negro Spirituals, Fisk Jubile Singers, 1872

Steal away
Steal away
Steal Away home to Jesus,
Steal away
Steal away home
I aint got long to stay here.
Folk Songs of the American Negro, 1907

Swing down Chariot stop and let me ride,
Swing sown chariot stop and let me ride
Rock me lord, rock me lord,
Calm and easy,
I got a home on the other side.
Unknown

♪

Swing low, sweet chariot,
Coming forth to carry me home
Swing low, sweet chariot,
Coming forth to carry me home
Unknown

Singing these songs (that were actually coded messages used by slaves) brings us back to the slave experience and the reality of their never-ending struggle to be free. The songs connect them to our present efforts to overcome racism in America, and to remain strong no matter what. They let us know that as African people we are a tribe with traditions and a commitment that comes from our history and heritage.

THE QUICK HITS—CENTRO MUST HAVES

❖ Big glass of water
❖ Cross (in water)
❖ Florida water
❖ Rum
❖ Honey
❖ Cigars
❖ Lucky leaves
❖ Flowers
❖ Bible
❖ Prayer book
❖ Incense
❖ White candles
❖ Oils or perfumes
❖ White tablecloth

Oh yeah, if you have never been to a centro you are probably wondering what the cigar is for. People will tell you different things like, we are on Native American territory and they liked tobacco. Partially, this is true. But the fact is that one of the best incenses that can be used for spiritual cleaning is tobacco. And spiritualists, including women, often heighten their spiritual openness when smoking cigars.

CHAPTER III
THE ORISHAS

MI EGUN

The understanding of Orisha must begin with Egun. But first, what is Orisha? In my simplest explanation, Orisha are deities and nature's forces that assist in doing the work of Olofi (God), and they help to guide our path on earth. Orisha can be seen in many aspects of God's creations – oceans, rivers, volcanoes, mountains, trees, stones, etc., as such the Yoruba are nature worshipping people. Orisha are in many ways God's helpers much like the saints are in Catholicism, or the gods in Greek Mythololgy.

One of the primary Orisha we worship is called Egun. I mentioned previously, that the term *egun* is referred to as the dead, or ancestors, or specific spirits around us (little e). The word *Egun* is also referred to as the Orisha Egun (Big E). Orisha Egun is the collective embodiment of the dead that make up your entire spirit existence. Big Egun is like your spirit DNA. It is an ancestral heritage collective of all that is a part of you – African-American, Yoruba, Panamanian, European, Native American, a godchild, a priest from a particular ocha lineage, an enslaved African crossing the middle passage, a queen or king upon her throne – all that. All That. Its all those Eguns that belong to you or support you, rolled in one. Whereas the eguns (spirits – little e) we connect with at our obobera are very specific, (we often know their names, or can discover their names), Orisha Egun represents those which we know, and those which we do not know. It's much more all encompassing in practice. It's the Antoine Fisher family reunion of all your Eguns; *it's the who that be Mabel family reunion?* In worshipping Big Egun, you have them all together, drinking dranks, breaking bread, and smoking the pipe! All in your honor, no doubt. And when all the Eguns are working together for your life, that's some strong power.

Yoruba believe in reincarnation. In principle, Egun recognizes the sacredness of the entire cycle of being alive and then dead and then alive again. And perhaps one day when we have paid our dues and passed the test, of evolving out of one cycle to another level, it is Egun who will open the door. Therefore, Egun is the Orisha of continuity through ancestry. It is the Orisha that declares, "what is dead is never dead." Importantly, Egun is the principle of the cycle of humanity that includes the dead and the living. Without being able to commune and relate to the unseen world of spirits and Orisha - and through them to Olofi, we would have no religion. Egun is the medium; the door we have to pass through to get to Orisha. Therefore we must honor Egun before any other Orisha. So how do we do this?

The first thing is we establish, the Oju Egun, a permanent shrine to our Egun. At this shrine we call out in prayer the names of the deceased people in our blood line and Orisha family line. We also acknowledge in our prayers, all those whose names we do know. This establishes the collective that is the active presence of Egun. In Nigeria there is a very popular practice known as Egungun, a masquerade that appears publicly on specific occasions and dances with an entourage of drummers and singers all around the town. The masquerade connects the entire community to the world of the dead. This masquerade is a part of the Egun shrine in Nigeria.

When African slaves found themselves in Cuba, the Egungun (masquerade) aspect of worship could not be enacted because by its physical appearance, the spectacle would reveal their forbidden African practices. Yet understanding that honoring Egun still was absolutely necessary to Orisha worship, the Egungun public dancing ceremony was simply dropped. Yet the real Egun shrine itself was not forgotten, but was often kept hidden in a small shed outside of the house. In Cuba, when the African slaves saw where the Cubans went for a piss or a dump, you know, the outhouse, they were amazed that it looked sort of looked like their Oju Egun space back in Africa. So basically the enslaved African priests built similar structures to keep their Egun shrine, because they knew the slave captors would never look inside of a slave shit hole, since they thought it was just a toilet. The result? Survival! Generations later, many practitioners having had no understanding of the real reason why Egun was kept in a structure similar to an outhouse, and now living in modern houses and apartments, still practiced keeping their Oju Egun shrine in the bathroom. However, bit by bit, African Americans, and Latinos as well, began to realize that, no longer being slaves, we could put our Oju Eguns in other places. Nowadays many of us designate a special corner, closet, or, place in the kitchen to set up our Oju Egun shrine. This is usually kept in a separate space from your obobera and other Orisha shrines.

There are two parts to the Egun shrine. The first part is a designated space delineated by a chalk half-circle on the floor, with a glass of water inside the space. Along with this, there is a stick that has been ritually washed, fed, prayed to and perhaps decorated with colorful cloths and maybe carved a bit. It is slowly tapped on the floor while mentioning the name of each ancestor, and when singing or praying to Egun it is tapped on the floor more rapidly. The stick (Opa Egun), is really like a symbolic version of Egungun. It is used to call egun to the order of Egun and to ritually be danced during Egun bembes.

In terms of offerings, the main staples for this shrine are whatever food is consumed in your house. Sometimes flowers are added depending on your house rule (some say that flowers are only for spirits), leaves (rhododendrons, sometimes called "lucky leaves"), and a glass of water should always be there even if there is no food. Following Lucumi tradition there should also be a cigar, rum, and black coffee. What you give will change from day to day, but generally you change the plates of food whenever you eat in your house. Now this made sense to me. In Bed-Stuy, when I used to hang out in the neighborhood with my crew, we would always pour out on the sidewalk a little soda or beer for the homey who wasn't there anymore—dead but not gone, always remembered.

THE QUICK HITS—EGUN SHRINE

❖ Praise: Laiye Laiye Omo Lewa Omo Laiye, Laiye Laiye Omo Lewa Omo Laiye

❖ **Number:** nine

❖ **Colors:** nine colored cloths, multicolored

❖ **Day:** Everyday

❖ **Special Stuff:** Opa Egun (stick), mask, flowers, lucky leaves, white candles, 9 colored candles

❖ **Special Food:** glass of water, all foods, san cocha, pork, black coffee, rum

❖ **Domain:** kitchen floor, bathroom floor, shed outside of house

Mi Elegba

Elegba is the Orisha of the crossroads. He is also known as Eshu. He is the Orisha that helps you to make a decision when you are stuck and can't figure out which way to turn. Elegba is the first Orisha we go to for guidance, or for blessings. Elegba is considered Olofi's messenger. Whenever you want to talk to another Orisha, you first speak to or acknowledge Elegba so that things will go smoothly for you. This is because Elegba is also known as the trickster. He will sometimes play jokes on you, so it is good to know your Elegba, so that you can discern when he is being serious about something and when he is not.

Elegba likes all kinds of candies, toys, and sweet stuff. You can practically give anything to Elegba because he has an insatiable appetite. His colors are red and black, and his special number is three or seven. Elegba's special day is Monday. Because Elegba is a world Orisha, he likes to do things that will take him outside. Actually, the Elegba in our homes is an aspect of Eshu. My godmother says that Elegba is the controlled force that we can bring into our house, while Eshu is more uncontrolled and therefore lives outside in the world. When we are in the streets, especially late at night, it good to leave something for Eshu—pennies, small candies, anything he likes. You can leave these things on corners or tossed into crossroads and pray for safety while moving about in his domain.

During my high school years, I had more fights than most people. Growing up in Bed-Stuy, you had to act—no, be hard to some extent. When someone would say the wrong thing to me, I'd be quick to jump bad. My frame was skinny, but my mouth was my biggest asset. I could curse with the best of them, and I talked a lot of shit, so I was easily able to intimidate people. Obviously not everyone, because as I mentioned, I did get into a lot of fights.

Part of the fighting was because I really had fear, yet I was not about to let that side of me show. I had to do it quickly. So instead of wasting a lot of time breaking, I would just throw my hands up and go for it because I knew the more I argued, the more the fear factor could kick in.

One of the biggest fights I had was during my sophomore year at Erasmus Hall High School. My school was located in the Flatbush section of Brooklyn. During the eighties, there was large influx of Carribean people moving into this area. One afternoon, in my gym class, this girl from Jamaica threw a big blue medicine ball at me which hit me directly in the head, knocking me down. When I looked over, she was smiling; I got up, looked her dead-on, and waited for some sort of apology. She had the nerve to still have a big stupid grin on her face. I took steps toward her to make sure she understood where I was coming from. I guess my posse—the six B girls (I was Bounty)—could see that things were getting heated up because before I could get to her, they had already intervened and began pounce on her behind. I didn't get to land a punch. A small white woman gym teacher jumped in to stop the fight and got beat up in the process. It was absolute mayhem. In all of this, I was suspended and deemed to be a ringleader of a gang and branded a troublemaker. My mom came up to the school and met with the guidance counselor, Jamaican Girl, who happened to be a senior, and me. I can still hear my mother fussing, "Oh, Kemba, how could you fight a senior?" I thought, *Whatever, Mom. She's a high school senior not a senior citizen – give me a break.* In the discussion, I must have said something smart and rolled my eyes at the guidance counselor, because out of nowhere my mother slapped me dead across the face, right in front of Jamaican Girl. Oooh, I had never been so pissed off in my life. All I could think of was how I hated my mother for disrespecting me in front of the girl. When I looked up, Jamaican Girl had that same stupid smirk on her face, like she had when she hit me with the ball; if I could have gotten up and knocked the mess out of her, I would have, but I was always afraid of my mother's temper—she was the law.

When we got home, I was pissed and stayed in my room, but I did have someone I could go to. That was my Elegba. I had received my warriors—Elegba and Ogun—a couple of years after I received my *illekes*. For me it was the best thing, because it finally meant I could do something. I begged Elegba to make them all pay—oh, but not my mother, of course not. I had faith in my warriors, especially Elegba.

They say Elegba is close to kids, and I guess I quickly became in tuned with that. My Elegba was made in a conch shell, with a mouth formed by cowrie shells; my brother's Elegba was made of coral reef with lines and groves looking more like a big ol' brain. I marveled at how they matched us up perfectly—I was the big mouth; he was the intellect.

My Super smart older brother Ketema, ibae.

Almost immediately after receiving my warriors, I established a relationship with my Elegba. I would talk to him and give him stuff like candy, toys, honey, rum, and cigars. Giving the rum was always the worst part because you had to spit it on Elegba and my mouth would burn like hell. I was told we spit because the ase (power) from our own mouth mixed with the rum makes the offering more powerful.

My godmother gave me my Mojubas, (*prayers asking for praise to God, Egun, and the Orisha*), to say before talking to my warriors and taught me how to throw obi to them. Thowing obi is one system we use to receive yes or no reponses to our questions from our Orisha. This is done using four pieces of coconut, and is taught by one's godparent. This was my first real step to communicating with my Elegba, and Elegba communicating back to me. It took me some time getting used to throwing obi; I often had to call on my mother for assistance because I was stuck or couldn't remember a certain step. I longed to become a skilled obi thrower like she was, and to recite the Mojubas without looking at my notes. It took a lot of practice to memorize them; yet for many years **I would keep my handwritten notes right next to me when it came time to talk to my warriors.**

One of my memorable Elegba moments was when I was a teen; I had a tiny crush on this boy, Barry. He lived in Brevoort Projects. Well anyway, after a party at his house, I went on the roof with him to just chill. We sort of got caught up kissing a little bit, but that was the most of it. By Monday, Barry had told everyone at his high school that he and I had had sex. So untrue! I was still a virgin, and plus I had a boyfriend (OK, so I should not have been making out with someone else, true…anyway back to the point). I didn't attend Barry's school, but my cousin Yolanda and my best friend Kateria did, so I got the word. Even my boyfriend, the Almighty Johnny Dee (or just John) got the word, but he knew it was a lie. Anyway, I went to my Elegba and

47

told him what had happened. I asked him to give this guy hell until he apologized to me for lying.

Many months went by before I saw Barry again at a school football game and of course by then the nonsense had died down. When he saw me, he couldn't even look me in the eye. After a while, he meekly came over and said he was sorry for lying on me. I smiled, thinking I couldn't believe this tall wannabe- yet good looking thug homeboy was over here apologizing to me all humbly. Then I suddenly remembered my conversation with Elegba, and I was like, "Yeah, yeah, my Elegba is the bomb!" I don't actually know if Barry's life had been crumbling all those months, but I would like to think it was.

Later, my ojubona, Mama Monique, would tell me that we do not use Elegba or any Orisha to do harm to people. We have them to assist our lives, but not to do harm to others. She said when you go to Orisha to ask them to do wrong to someone else, you are insulting them, and your curse will come back on you. Orisha knows what you need, and all people are their children; it is not your place to pray for their punishment. I'm sure she was right. At the time though, I was still hoping Elegba had exacted some good penalty on Barry's lying behind. Anyway, work that Elegba; he loves young people and will do just about anything for them.

APATAKI (ADAPTATION)

Two best friends, Marley and Robo, did everything together. They played ball together, swam together, went to the same school, and even had dinner at one another's house on many occasions. They were so close and would often remark, "We are the best of friends, and nothing can ever break us apart." One day while they were boasting to some people on the street about their special bond, Elegba happened to be passing by and heard their declaration. "Oh really?" Elegba said to himself. He laughed and decided to play a little trick on them to test their friendship.

The next day the two best friends were walking down the block. As they walked, a most unusual-looking man passed right between them. When they were sure the man could not hear them, they each burst out laughing.

"Dang, did you see that guy? He looked like a straight joker," said Marley.

"Yeah," Robo agreed. "Dressed in those crazy-ass clothes."

"And why was he painted all red?" Marley said.

"Hey, what are you talking about? That man was painted all black," Robo blurted.

"He was not," Marley retorted. "He was all red."

Robo looked at Marley like he was bugging—he again told Marley that the man was all black; it was clear and plain to see. Marley and Robo began to argue; each knew what he had seen and was not backing down. Marley accused Robo of having eyesight problems just like his mama. Robo told Marley that he must be suffering from mental problems since it ran in his family. Before long, the arguing turned into a brawl. Each was throwing blows, cursing, and swearing. People ran out their homes to break up the fight, and couldn't believe their eyes when they saw Robo and Marley fighting. "Not the inseparable friends," people shouted over the melee. Marley and Robo both announced their newly formed dislike for each other, and till this day, they are no longer friends. Point: don't be so absolute about anything. Elegba painted half his body red and the other half black to confuse and start the argument. When you think you know everything, life will trick you, and you will learn that you do not know anything. Humble yourself—learn to bend and yield. Elegba is everywhere.

THE QUICK HITS—ELEGBA STATS

❖ **Praise:** Elegba Bara Bara Kikenye Laroye

❖ **Also Known As:** Eshu

❖ **Number:** three or seven

❖ **Colors:** red and black

❖ **Day:** June 13

❖ **Special Stuff:** Garabato (Elegba stick), toys, marbles, coins

❖ **Special Food:** toasted corn, palm oil, rum, gin, fish and jutia, potato cakes, all food

❖ **Domain:** front door, back door, front of house, outside, streets

❖ **Don't** walk diagonally across intersections. If you do, leave something for Eshu/Elegba.

❖ **Give** offerings of pennies, candies, at the corners for Elegba/Eshu.

Mi Ogun

"Praise the Red, the black and the green
Brothers and sisters are being redeemed
Open up your eyes and see
We are on our way to being free."
Uhuru Sasa Shule theme song

Some say that the world itself was born in violence. You know, the big bang theory. Yoruba scripture says that too. And that the residue of the primordial explosion is the earth itself. Ogun. The metaphorical reference for that is iron..said to be the oldest matter. That's why some say that Ogun is the oldest Orisha. In modern times, Ogun still rules over violence. Both good and bad. Good like the surgeon's knife, or that slick new car (engine made of iron) or the beams of a skyscraper. Bad like the madman's arsenal of guns, and the single grenade used to kill many, indiscriminately.

Ogun is often seen as a tough Orisha. He is a hunter and a fighter. We say that if we have a battle to fight, **we need to give the problem to Ogun so that he will fight our battles for us.** However, Ogun is also good-natured. He is a kind and very generous Orisha.

Ogun is noted as the Orisha that carved out civilization in the world. He is the carpenter; he is the police. he is the blacksmith. Blacksmiths are actually considered to be Ogun's most natural priests. Before, the world was uninhabitable, and then Ogun provided a way for us to live on the land. Ogun is responsible for the advancement of technology and industrialization. Because of this, people often go to Ogun when they are in need of work and ask him to provide a way.

When I was younger, I did not go to Ogun as often as I went to Elegba. I probably should have, as it would have surely prevented me from getting into so many fights. When I received Ogun full later in life (ask your godparent what I mean by this), I was told not to pick up any of Ogun's tools to do battle with anyone. This included guns and knives. Not picking up a gun was easy, but I cringed at the thought of not being able to carry a knife, as it was the homegirl weapon of choice growing up in the Eighties in New York City. Not that I used one on anybody, really, but everyone had a switchblade for protection back in the day. Times have changed now, and the thought of a young person carrying a weapon today is frightening. I guess it was scary for parents back then as well.

When I reflect on all the people I knew who died tragically, having been shot or stabbed, it's overwhelming. In my senior year of high school, which was now Samuel J. Tilden HS, a young freshmen football player, Martin Boulay, was stabbed down the block from the school and died on the spot. I saw his lifeless body lying there on that hard concrete street. Later in the same year, Cheryl Edwards, a girl who played spades with me during lunch, was stabbed and killed right in front of the school;

they tried to rob her for her earrings. My friends and I cried—she was a good person and her mother's only child.

Throughout my teen years, violence with guns and knives was rampant in my community. Every teenager I knew growing up in New York City had been in numerous gun shootouts where everyone was either hitting the floor or running wildly. These incidents usually took place at someone's house party, at a spot, or one of the summer block parties we used to have in Brooklyn. In truth, the shootouts were occurring all over the place—in school, on the block, at the park—everywhere. It seemed thrilling sometimes, but when close friends and people I used to chill with started getting killed by this senseless violence, the excitement wore off very quickly.

It turned into something even uglier when one of the people who died because of violence was my family. My little brother Italo was shot taking a shortcut through a neighborhood schoolyard park. Although he seemingly recovered fully, he died months later from a massive intestinal blockage caused as a result of the injuries he sustained from the shooting. Italo was a rising basketball star, and a truly gifted young man. He knew a lot about black history, and was quick to draw you into a trivia match to test your wits against his. Italo's sixteen years on this side was short, but his presence is everlasting, for as we know of Egun, one never really dies.

Me and my younger brother Italo, ibae

During that time period, my little brother was only one of several people I knew who died as a result violence. Famed civil rights activist Sonny Carson, ibae (my other self-appointed godfather) brought Tupac Shakur, ibae to come out and speak to the young people about the senseless killings going on. Tupac was instrumental in helping ease some of the tensions that were permeating around our neighborhood. Ironically, less than two years later, Tupac would die from this same kind of tragic violence.

Nothing can erase that kind of pain from any family's life. I have known so many people who have died because of violence that I've almost lost count. But I have never forgotten any of them; sometimes I'd wonder what their lives would be like now if they had lived to see twenty or even thirty. During my years at Uhuru Sasa Shule, one of the central points the mwalimu (teachers) instilled in the students was that we must be prepared to fight our enemies. We were a black militant group in so many ways. Most of our class trips were actually school demonstrations against social injustice, police brutality, and boycotts against racist establishments. **And while we marched through the streets, we sang songs of black pride laced with the names of our African histories greatest people, past and present:** Malcolm X, Marcus Garvey, H. Rap Brown, Kwame Nkrumah, Queen Mother Moore, Martin Luther King, Jr., Nat Turner, Steven Biko, W.E.B. Dubois. Sekou Toure, George Washington Carver, Queen Nzinga, Al Vann, Assata Shukur and countless others. Although we were taught that we needed to be ready for war, we did not learn physical combat, except for the occasional self-defense karate lessons. Our weapon was our mind; the mwalimu wanted to make sure we knew how to think, plan and strategize, or as one of our common saying went, we needed to get ready to *educate, agitate, and organize*. Similarly, Ogun would not want young people to use his tools for battle, but instead use their minds.

This makes Ogun so necessary in my life. I need Ogun to protect me in the world. Also, Ogun says, "Let me fight your battles." How important for me to remember, because in anger and through rage I could pick up a weapon and regret my actions for the rest of my life. Through Ogun, I am calmed to know that I am being protected. In saying this, I know that I still must live wisely—which means not deliberately putting myself in dangerous situations. I can't start mess and then say, "I know you got my back, Ogun," because it might be me who will pay the ultimate price.

APATAKI (ADAPTATION)

In many ways Kwesi was your typical guy. He loved to make things. You would always find him in his garage sawing and nailing things together. He was good at making furniture, bookcases, and stuff like that. He also loved to forge and weld iron and other metals. People would ask him to make iron doors or put bars on their windows; he even knew how to make jewelry.

When Kwesi wasn't doing this you could find him mowing the lawn, digging weeds out the flowerbeds, or chopping away at some trees. Pretty much Kwesi loved to do things with his hands. He was very skilled at creating things. There was only one problem: for all the energy Kwesi put into creating, he never really learned how to socialize. He always seemed standoffish to people. Plus he looked so serious all of the time; his nature sort of frightened people, so although they asked for his help, they never really invited him over to their homes or to their parties. Kwesi didn't care because he didn't really see the need to be around people anyway.

Well, up the street lived this girl, Zenobia. She liked Kwesi, but as with most people, he never paid any attention to her. Zenobia had a discussion with her big sister Yema, and then set out to get Kwesi to love her. She began running through the neighborhood. Her jogging suit was gold, with a streak of red up the sides. It fit her nicely, hugging her curvaceous breasts, hips, and butt. Instead of braiding her hair down, she did just the opposite. She unraveled it and let it flow all thick and wild over her head. Zenobia would jog several miles, then stop in front of Kwesi's house to drink her water. She kept the water in a gold metallic water bottle. Panting heavily, then slowing her breath, Zenobia would drink incessantly from her bottle. The water would drip down her mouth and chin and down onto her chest right above her sweat suit. She would very slowly wipe away the water mixed with her sweat, and fling her hands to the wind.

This practice carried on for several days. On the fifth day, Kwesi looked up from his workshop and took notice. He stared at Zenobia for what seemed like an eternity. When she jogged away, his eyes never left her. The next few days, this ritual continued; Zenobia would end her jogging in from of Kwesi's house, drink her water, and leave Kwesi staring after her. After she jogged off, Kwesi found himself thinking about her all day. On day ten, Kwesi decided to greet Zenobia. Zenobia played coy at first. She acted like she wasn't interested. This did not deter Kwesi. When Zenobia came running in front of his house the next day, Kwesi asked her if he could join her. She allowed him to. When the run was over, Zenobia offered Kwesi some of her water. Kwesi gladly drank from her bottle; the water was sweet and like nothing Kwesi had ever tasted before. He looked at Zenobia and knew he was in love. From then on, Zenobia took Kwesi with her to all the parties and events. After a while, people got to know him better, and realized what a cool guy he was. And thanks to Zenobia, Kwesi actually began to enjoy being around people as well.

This was an adaptation of the apataki where Oshun entices Ogun out of the forest.

Ogun is the patron Orisha of the Egbe Iwa Odo Kunrin & Egbe Iwa Odo Binrin, a youth-rites-of-passage organization out of New York, with members in various cities. This picture is part of the ceremony of the teenage men being sworn in. In the far right is the founder Iya Oloriwaa. Notice the machete in her hand, Ogun's main tool.

THE QUICK HITS—OGUN STATS

❖ **Praise:** Ogun Owanile'O Ogun Kubu Kubu

❖ **Number:** three or seven

❖ **Colors:** green, green and black, red, black, and green

❖ **Day:** June 29

❖ **Special Stuff:** raffia, machetes

❖ **Special Food:** palm oil, plantains, bananas

❖ **Domain:** front door, forest

MI OCHOSI

Ochosi is the Orisha of good luck and fortune. He is brother to Ogun and Elegba, and also lives out in the woods. One of Ochosi's symbols is the bow and arrow. Ochosi is about truth and justice, so much so that if you've done something wrong, Ochosi is not the Orisha to help you get out of a sticky situation. If you are right, and I do mean correctomundo, then Ochosi will save you from unjust situations, but if you are wrong he will hang your butt (figuratively speaking, I think). He believes in following the rules of the law and following the rules of institutions one belongs to. Like Ogun, he is associated with the police. He is also seen as the judge.

There is an *apataki* about Ochosi shooting an arrow through his mother because she was guilty of taking the yams Ochosi had gathered for Obatala (Principal Yoruba deity; father of all Orishas). When there was no explanation for the missing yams, Ochosi shot his arrow into the sky and said, "Please let it hit the guilty person responsible." He had no idea it would be his own mother. Thus Ochosi is also known as the Orisha that can bring about instant death.

However, Ochosi is also about love. He is known to move with lightning speed, directness, and the ability to fly. Depending on what is being sought, Ochosi arrows can bring instant love or produce instant death. Truth always wins with Ochosi. A lot of times, people go to Ochosi when they are seeking direction in their life.

APATAKI (ORIGINAL)

Zelda believed that she could get away with boosting items from her favorite clothing store. She shopped there frequently, spending hundreds of dollars on several occasions. What did it matter if she occasionally put a blouse in her bag without paying? It was easy to do. The store didn't have any alarms on their clothes, and she knew that the mirrors in the dressing room were not two-way mirrors. So this became her normal routine. She'd spend fifty or hundred dollars on some clothes, then put one item in her oversized bag. Zelda did this for over a year. It became normal to her. She told a few friends about her good fortune.

After a year passed, one of the friends that she had told got a job working at the very store she boosted from. Zelda had completely forgotten the conversation she had had earlier with the friend, but the friend had not. To get in good favor, the friend told the manager about Zelda boosting from the store. The manger had store security waiting for Zelda when she left the dressing room. They of course, discovered a stolen pair of jeans in her bag. Because the jeans cost over two hundred dollars, the store manager called the police, and Zelda was arrested. They walked her through the mall in handcuffs; everyone found out. Through others, Zelda discovered that her friend had blown the whistle on her. She was furious. She went to her warriors and begged that justice be done. What a treacherous friend! She asked Elegba, Ogun, and Ochosi to please help her.

In a short time, Zelda had to appear in court for her charges. The judge stated that because she had been boosting for some time, he would not show any leniency towards her. The judge sentenced Zelda to one year in jail and a one-thousand-dollar fine for her offense. It was the maximum punishment for her crime. To Zelda and many others, it seemed like a harsh sentence. Even to Elegba and Ogun it was heavy-handed. To Ochosi, it was justice. Period. *Do not ask Ochosi to help you if you are wrong; he will not rationalize your way of thinking.*

THE QUICK HITS—OCHOSI STATS

❖ **Praise:** Ochosi Ode Mata Mata Se

❖ **Number:** three or seven

❖ **Day:** April 23

❖ **Color:** blue

❖ **Special Stuff:** bow and arrow, deer skin, deer head, armor

❖ **Special Food:** birdseed

❖ **Special Drink:** anisette

Mi Osun

Oh the warm mellow sunlight is shining
And the trees like great sentinels stand
They are guarding our dear alma mater
The pride of Virginia land
Excerpt Virginia State University Song

Osun is the guardian Orisha. He watches over us at all times. Osun stands perched on one leg, yet he is the soldier that never sleeps. He is always on guard; he is always awake. Osun is one of the Orisha that makes up the warriors, along with Elegba, Ogun, and Ochosi. Osun watches out for Iku (death). In our prayers, we always ask Osun to warn us if Iku is around. When we are frightened in our homes, we can take our Osun and shake the bells throughout the house. This is to ward off Iku in the home.

Osun has a special connection to the Orisha Osain, who deals with medicines and herbs. In our tradition, Osun is often received from a babalowo, a priest of Ifa, although a male santero, *(a full Yoruba initiate)*, can give an Osun to someone as well. One *apataki* says that Osun was called to watch over the wife of Obatala, the father of all Orisha, but he fell asleep and Obatala's wife was raped. From that point on, he was destined to keep watch at all times.

In my home, Osun is kept up high so that there is no chance he will be knocked over. Because Osun is the watchman, he is never to be tipped or knocked over; when this happens, you must do a special *ebo*, or offering.

THE QUICK HITS—OSUN STATS

❖ **Praise:** Osun bole ma de bole, dodo ganga labosi, Osun bole ma de bole, dodo ganga labosi awo

❖ **Also Known As:** the Watchman

❖ **Special Stuff:** efun, cocoa butter

❖ **Special Food:** fruit, green grapes

❖ **Special Place:** Placed up high in the home

Teen Obatala priest Marquis

MI OBATALA

Obatala is the father of all Orisha. He is the highest of all the Orisha. Sometimes, Obatala is depicted as an old, wise man; at other times he is a young, gallant warrior. He is the owner of the white cloth and the owner of all heads. Everyone must pay big respect to this Orisha. I have always considered Obatala as my first Orisha father. I received my *illekes* for Obatala, so he has always been governing over me. In fact, in most *iles*, or houses/communities of people who have the same godparent, if a person doesn't know who the Orisha of their head is, they are considered to belonging to Obatala. This goes to show you the reverence people have for Obatala in this tradition.

Before I had Ocha or any other Orisha, I had to go in my mother's Ocha room and salute her Obatala. Along with her countless godchildren, this is a simple act we still practice today. Equally significant is the fact that my godmother has Obatala crowned, too. I, along with my many godsisters and godbrothers, make it a habit to *dobale (salute)* before Obatala whenever we go to our godmother's house. That's just the way it is. Simple practices like this are the foundation stones in our everyday life. It is no wonder that my Ocha *ile* has steadily grown over the course of four decades because of the example set by my mother and godmother - two exemplary Obatala priests.

When one is divining to a person's Obatala, everyone must kneel in respect. During a drumming, when they sing to Obatala, you will notice that everyone, regardless of what Orisha they have crowned, will touch the floor. When we do this, it is a sign of respect for that particular Orisha.

As I grew up, Obatala had always been a fascinating Orisha to me. During those days, Obatala was the only Orisha I had heard of that could be either male or female. I pondered on what attributes of Obatala could constitute him as being identified as both sexes. It made me think of homosexual or transgender people. Were they more likely to be children of Obatala? The years of being around people initiated in Ocha has dispelled that notion. Gay and transgender people can be connected with any Orisha. Nevertheless, Obatala is an exalted Orisha, the Orisha of never-ending wisdom. He is the Orisha of good reasoning and intellect. He is the owner of the heads.

Obatala can be patient with his children but will also teach them lessons so they may grow in life. Obatala is about righteousness and morality. Because the white cloth is so essential, Obatala is associated with always wanting to have impeccable white clothes. My godmother would say, "Take heed: the obsession with perfection could be a downfall, because nothing is perfect in the world. Sometimes you have to learn to accept things that you cannot change because it is what it is, period." Obatala is about remaining cool in the world and learning balance.

My godmother, Mama Stephanie. A true scholar on Orisha practice, she has almost forty years of Obatala and has taught countless people about this religion.

A STORY BEGINNING - SOFT HEAD

Prologue

On the 28th of April, she came into this world. Truth be as it is, it was an easy journey. But the road ahead was hard. Unkind and unsettling, like mud under feet, never quite being able to stand firm. Always sinking just a little. Sliding to the left; sliding to right. That's why twenty-two years later, to the very day, she made her exit back. *Ain't* nobody even know. Just here today, and you know the rest. When she got back, the first person she wanted to see was the headmaker. Boy did she have some choice words for him. "Hey O". I'm back she shouted outside his door. "Who in the world name is that?" O wondered. "Hey O, I Know you hear me calling you, I said I'm back", she blurted again. It took O a few minutes to recognize the voice, but then it came back to him. "My goodness, that's Nara." "What is she doing back here already."? O felt genuinely puzzled. O came out of his home, and greeted Nara with the customary bow; one befit for the princess daughter of a king. Nara looked at O, and blared out, "what the big idea giving me a soft head". "I couldn't do anything with it." Yeah she was one of those softheads alright. When she picked it, O knew there was going to be problems. It just didn't seem like the right thing for someone like her – of royal ancestral and all. But Nara insisted. To her it was pretty and she liked pretty things. O reminded Nara, "look you picked the softhead; I gave you other options, but you were adamant on that one." "Yeah, but why didn't you tell me how much trouble a softhead was going to have. I mean nothing seemed to work out, and when it did, I had to work double as hard for it", declared Nara. "Look here"', O replied, I wanted you to get a stronger head. I knew the hard head would be able to take the punches and keep on rolling. You had a choice before you went. You made the pick." Nara retorted, "Yeah, but you didn't tell me, that a soft head was going to struggle so." "Truth as it is, little Ms. Nara, all the heads struggle. You are right though; the soft heads have it a little bit more difficulty. Ha! But usually they don't even know it. I'm surprised to see you back here so soon. What happened?? You know what Nara said, "I just decided to say to hell with it; I'd already spent too much time with this head and it wasn't getting me anywhere. So I'm back now – I want to trade this one in for another." O looked at Nara not surprising, and let out nice big laugh. He had seen this before. It wasn't a common thing though; most people just worked with what they had; they learned to survive despite their heads. "Nara, what did you do to get back? It was not your time." "I took a punch of pills, and went to sleep. That's all." "Mmmmm", O remarked. "well here's the situation Nara; I can not give you another head. You have to make the one you have work for you. "No" cried Nara. "Yes, you do," replied O. "Come on, just switch this one out – what's the big deal?" "I can't do it Nara, sorry. Big O forbids the switching of heads that have not completed their mission." "What. Why.. give me a break. Please O, do it for me," Nara begged. "I wont do it Nara. You need to get your soft head together and turn back around now." Nara looked at O as is she wanted to beat him with all her might, but she knew that he was untouchable. There was no way to really get to him. She looked at him with anger. "Well, I'm sure enough not going back, Nara snorted. I'm going to see my grandma, great grandpappy, and my cousin Selojka now. With that she started to take a few paces in the direction of her ancestral homelands. O stopped her still. "You can't go." "Why not, Nara cried. Because you did not finish what you were called to do. Incompletion unacceptable. "Are you trying to tell me I can't go and be with my people now. "Yes that's I what I am telling you, Nara. You cannot go to them until everything you are to do is done. "What am I supposed to do then, this really sucks. Seriously, what am

I supposed to, O. "You are going back." "I don't want to; I just want to go and be with my family", cried Nara. "No Nara, I am sorry, but you can not go to them. However, when you go back, they can still come to you. Make sure you receive them and treat them well." "You told me that before, but I hardly ever saw them," Nara retorted. "Pay attention this time, Ms. Nara. They come all ways," O gently remarked as he nudged Nara towards the forest from which she had just arrived. "So I must go back, and I must go with this same soft head.?"

"Yes. And do not curse the head you have. It is yours. Make it work for you." But I have nowhere to go anymore, remember O. I took the pills. It is done. The form is already breaking down. "You will start again. You will go, with your softhead, and start again." Nara screamed, "Oh you are so cruel to me O. Please don't do this to me. "Get ready now Nara. Until you complete what you were sent to do, you will only get as far as me." "Not true! I should have gone straight to my Grandma's house. Oh why did I come here first?"

"This was the only stop you could have made. Now it's time to turn around. Do well this time Nara, so that you do not have to repeat your life. Goodbye little princess daughter of kings. "Oh, this is some bullshit, O." "Out of that dung you speak, make some beautiful flowers grow sweet Nara. Peace be with you", replied O.

The head you carry is the one you chose and it is yours to use. May you learn to use it wisely this time around.

This is an excerpt from a short story I am currently working on.

THE QUICK HITS—OBATALA STATS

❖ **Praise:** Hekua Baba Ochalembo Obatala Obataesa Obabatayana Ajaguna Legibo

❖ **Number:** eight

❖ **Colors:** white, silver (different roads may take a lil color with the white)

❖ **Day:** September 24

❖ **Special Stuff:** *efun, irukere,* elephant, knife/sword, white horse

❖ **Special Food:** white rice pudding, meringue, pears, green grapes,

❖ **Domain:** the mountain

Mi Yemonja

Yemonja is one of the most celebrated Orisha around the world. Considered the mother of all Orisha, Yemonja is the queen bee. She is a powerful Orisha. Many supplicate before her. In Brazil, millions of people pay homage to Yemonja on New Year's Day at Copacabana Beach. In New York, hundreds flock to the Yemonja Egbe's annual celebration to Yemonja at the ocean on Far Rockaway Beach.

Along with Olokun, Yemonja is represented by the ocean. Fishermen around the world pay homage to Yemonja, praying for protection, bountifulness, and permission to the Orisha of the seas they must navigate. When you think about the world being 66 percent water, you can better understand of the grandness of Yemonja. Her colors are all shades of blue, like the ocean. The beads in her ilekes are blue and crystal. A few of her symbols are seashells, fish, the crescent moon, and stars.

Me chillin' on the beach doing my favorite Yemonja pose.

Yemonja is associated with the mother—the matriarch. Drawings of Yemonja illustrate her with full breasts and wide hips. Yemonja is a gentle Orisha; she is caring, patient, and understanding. She has unconditional love for children. She is a protector of children, often fighting their battles. She can even be seen as overprotective. As such, Yemonja can also be depicted as a fighter. In some roads, she carries a machete and wears pants.

Baba Lloyd, my godfather and the patriarch of our Ocha house, is an initiated priest of Yemonja. Although he didn't make my Ocha, he did give me my ilekes and my warriors as a young girl. So for me, he will always have that special title in my life. After all, I am his *favorite* goddaughter (his godchildren are rolling their eyes right now...lol). Anyway, my godfather used to quip, "Yemonja is God." I guess he was speaking metaphorically, sort of like the Brooklyn five-percenters who all added "God Allah" to the end of their newly appointed names. It was a testament to how significant he saw Yemonja in the world.

Twenty-two years ago, when I was preparing to make Ocha, I did not know I would be getting initiated to Yemonja. At that time, I didn't know much about her and was not happy when I learned I would be making Yemonja. As a matter of fact, I cried like a fool. *Who is Yemonja? Why me?* All I knew was that she was the "Mother." That did not gel well with me. My own relationship with my mother was strained during my adolescent years, so I could see nothing good about being identified with the "Mother" Orisha.

I remember my mixed emotions—happy to be making Ocha, yet disappointed in the Orisha that I was making. I was even more pissed off because my older godsister, Roxanne, who was being raised on my throne, was an Oshun. On my middle day, I remember looking at her in her beautiful gold dress and then looking down at my blue conquistador-looking dress and wanting to cry. Oh, my poor godmother and ojubona. I don't know how they could have stood me. After several days on the throne, I recall lazily daydreaming and looking up into the whiteness of my blue throne. Without really thinking, words rolled out my mouth: "You know what, I really don't mind being a Yemonja; I actually kind of like it." I guess Yemonja had a few days to work on me. But man, I looked over and saw my godmother crying bucket tears. I was thinking, *OK, what is your problem, lady?* She said it was the best thing she had heard me say since she made my Ocha a few days earlier. I was stunned. I hadn't realized I was being such a pain in the butt. It's funny, when you are in the moment you really can't see yourself, but godmother's emotional outburst resounded loudly with me.

Since then, I have never regretted making Yemonja, and have spent the years trying to learn more about her and represent her well in the world. After all, Yemonja is one of the best Orisha you can have—she is beauty and grace personified.

Yemonja Teen Priests Hassan and Michele
at the annual Yemonja Bembe at the beach
in Far Rockaway, Brooklyn, NY.

THE QUICK HITS—YEMONJA STATS

- **Praise:** Yemonja Asarabe Olokun

- **Numbers:** seven, fourteen, twenty-one

- **Color:** many shades of blue, white, and silver

- **Day:** September 7

- **Special Stuff:** silver bangles, crescent moon, oars, jewelry, flowers

- **Special Food:** molasses, coconut candy, fish, black grapes, plums, ram, watermelon

- **Domain:** the ocean, rivers

MI OSHUN

She told me to walk this way
Talk this way
Walk this way
Talk this way
Run DMC

Oshun is the Orisha of love. Oshun, Yeye, or Iyalode, as she is sometimes called, is associated with beauty, love, and sweetness in the world. Oshun is often referred to as the river goddess, and her main domain is not only the river, but also lakes, streams, creeks, and waterfalls. I often imagine the poet John Keats lying by a riverbank and musing over Oshun when he wrote the words "Beauty is truth, truth beauty. That is all ye know on earth, and all ye need to know." That's just it. Oshun is the truth and the embodiment of beauty, something that goes beyond physical and into the inner spirit of a person. She represents harmony in life.

Of all the Orisha, Oshun is the youngest, but she is one of the fiercest. Despite her reputation of being sweet, she is a warrior Orisha and can fight with the best of them. She protects her children and those she loves. She also does not take well to being slighted—she can be unforgiving. The elders say that when Oshun mounts her children and comes laughing to be wary—her laughter might mean something totally different from what we would expect. It's better that she comes crying!

Oshun's colors are shades of gold and yellow. Her special number is five; she loves pretty jewelry of gold, brass, and amber. Oshun is the Orisha of fertility and creation. When women are trying to get pregnant, they give offerings to Oshun and ask for her blessings. Many children of Oshun are very creative and are, often able to create magnificent wonders with their hands. They are known to be great cooks, sewers, beaders, and artists. The children of Oshun are natural born leaders—they have a way of getting people to do what they want them to do.

Oshun is also the Orisha of marriage. One of our house customs on the day before a bride is to get married is to bathe her in specially prepared Oshun water with sweet things, while praying for a beautiful marriage for the new couple. Oshun also plays a sacred part in the initiation of Santeros. Before the ceremony, each must visit Oshun at her river shores, where a special ceremony is conducted. It is as if the Orisha of fertility is giving her blessing for this new life to be born.

Although I received my *illekes* for Obatala, I spent many years thinking I was a child of Oshun. Actually, I am sure I was at some point. When it was time to make my Ocha, my *abuelo(grandfather)* in Ocha, Padrino Cheo, ibae (Obatala priest) told my godmother that Oshun and Yemonja were warring for my head. Because our *ile* had experienced similar history of this nature, my *abuelo* in Ocha told my godmother I had to be made Yemonja. At that time, it was like being hit with a brick. Later, I understood it better. Even so, I still knew Oshun loved me like her own. I am honored by the fact that Oshun has walked so closely with me all my life. Most people can't tell if I'm a daughter of Yemonja or Oshun.

My ojubona has Oshun crowned. As typical with many children of Oshun, I spent a good number of my teenage years hanging out in my ojubona's kitchen. I think the kitchen is a sacred place for Oshun—I've seen a lot of people permanently set up Oshun in a special place in their kitchen. My sister Manny who has Oshun crowned is one of the best cooks of Ocha food in the community; she learned everything she knows from her ojubona, Mama Wambui, ibae (Oshun priest). I believe that Oshun works through Manny when she is cooking, so everyone who eats her food knows it is touched with love, like in the movie *Like Water For Chocolate*. With Oshun in your life, all the sweetness of the world will be revealed.

Young Oshun priest, Naiyah with her ojubona, Mama Isoke, a priest of Oya.

THE QUICK HITS—OSHUN STATS

❖ **Praise:** Ore Yeye O!

❖ **Number:** five

❖ **Colors:** gold, yellow

❖ **Day:** September 8 or September 12

❖ **Special Stuff:** mirrors, fans, brass metals, gold bangles, gold bells, oars, peacock feathers

❖ **Special Food:** honey, flan, honey cakes, cantaloupes, oranges, goat, pineapples, cinnamon sticks, Champagne

❖ **Domain:** the river, waterfalls

PADRE

*There was no slowing down the panting rains and the luminous echo
that followed*
*Its breath steady fast and continuous. It tried to mesh with the droning
sounds of the house*
*But were too powerful and drowned it. Fast quick no break no pause
for breath he did not tire*
Faster quicker no breaking no pausing for breathing he does not tire
*And the thunder roared in the background like a low flame under a
black pot. Beat beat*
*Pulse beat splash pulse tap pat pat pat puddles ping ping ping. I vener-
ate his body. I* dobale *mine.*
Shango is erect.
*Shango owner of the double axed swords stands attention. I feel him
moving in getting closer*
But am unafraid of my father and my father's wife.
He that is life comes to give life.
*My father has many strong forceful intense gentle bold soothing noisy
life giving orgasms in the eve of the night and he should*
He is king.
*Oya and Oshun are happy. Many tears fall and moisten the soil. Or is
Oba crying?*
*The traveling giant his roar is heard behind the cloud. He is moving to
another city but he will be back.*
Maferefun Shango mi Baba
Go but do come back and see me again. I will be waiting.

-Kemba '02

MI SHANGO

Damn right I like the life I live!
The Notorious B.I.G.

Of all the Orisha known in the Yoruba religion, Shango is one of the grandest. Shango is king. My father in Ocha, Shango is a super-magna Orisha. Many people around the world, whether in the religion or not, know about or have heard of Shango. In Trinidad, their version of the religion is actually called Shango Baptist.

Shango shares a special friendship with Obatala. He is represented by fire, thunder, and lightning. He is the Orisha of flash: always dazzling and exciting. Carrying a double-headed axe, Shango is revered for his great physical strength. He is a fighter. In many illustrations, you will see Shango depicted as big and massive, with broad shoulders and arms. Yet according to Baba John Mason, in some early Yoruba stories, Shango was actually small in frame. Most people who have a close connection with Shango know he is an Orisha that always has your back.

Along with being a great warrior, Shango is also a master strategist and a fierce lover. Shango loves challenges. A charmer, he is known for his superb dancing abilities. Shango believes that everyone should enjoy life and have a zest for living. He does not believe in being down because there is always something to keep living for. "Live life to the fullest" is the refrain that comes to mind when I think of Shango. Shango's colors are red and white, and his number is six. Children of Shango are known to be great diviners.

The drums are also very sacred to Shango. At *bembes*, it is exciting when Shango mounts a person. He comes to earth with great ferocity seeming turbulent, and angry, he often brings happiness to the people. I find children of Shango to be absolutely fabulous, although they can display an air of arrogance and superiority. Unfortunately, they sometimes find themselves victims of a lot jealousy and envy because they have strong personalities. At times, children of Shango need to work on balancing their confidence with modesty. Yet some people will still not like them, regardless of their behavior. Such is the way in life.

In my personal life, Shango has saved me many times. I don't need to do much; he is always there for me. I find that I also have a special connection with children of Shango—my good friend Alex (Oriate and Shango priest) has Shango crowned, and I cannot count how many times he has guided me in the right direction. What he says just makes sense; as a true strategist, he lets me know that it's not about winning the battle but about winning the war. In its ultimate sense, you want to win—you want to be on top. His advice oftentimes leads me to my humblest state of being—a process very necessary in succeeding. I know my father Shango speaks through my friend Alex, and all of the children of Shango in my life. Thankfully, I am able to listen and rise to the occasion. Shango is a passionate Orisha. With Shango in your life, any- and everything is possible.

Godbrother Alex, Shango priest and oriate

SHANGO APATAKI

There was once a king so full of pride that he did not permit any visitors to kingdom. None of the town's people could mix with his servants. The king had a daughter who was always sick and he spent a lot of money trying to cure her. According to the witch doctors in the town, the daughter had the evil eye on her from another incarnation. One day the king sent for Orunmila so that he could see his daughter but since Orunmila was so far away, he told the king to bring his daughter to him. Since the king was so proud, he didn't go. However, a few days later, seeing that his daughter was not getting any better, the king realized he had no choice but to go to Orunmila's house. When the king entered Orunmila's house, he didn't realize that the ceiling was low and his crown fell, rolling down a staircase outside. The town's people were there so they took the king's crown and hid it. The king had to visit each person on foot to find his crown. *Humility being taught again and again – even in your grandness and your greatness, be humble.*

The Quick Hits—Shango Stats

- ❖ **Praise:** Shango Kawo Kabisile

- ❖ **Numbers:** six, twelve

- ❖ **Colors:** red, red and white, leopard

- ❖ **Day:** December 4

- ❖ **Special Stuff:** raffia, double-sided *oshe*, drums, fire, thunderstone

- ❖ **Special Food:** palm oil, red wine, green bananas, red apples, hot amala, sweet amala

- ❖ **Domain:** base of huge tree, thunder, lightning,

MI OYA

Oya is the Orisha of the wind. She is an Orisha that delves in both the world of the living and the world of the dead. She lives at the entrance of the cemetery. As Yoruba, whenever we pass a cemetery, we salute Oya by waving our hands over our heads and saying, "Hekua Hey Yansa, keep death away from me." This is a ritual my mother had me and my brothers and sisters doing from a young age, and we have now passed it down to our children.

Oya has a very special connection with Egun; she is one of the few Orisha that can be worshiped right alongside Egun because she deals in the earthly and spirit world. Her magical powers are connected with life and death itself.

Oya is considered to be a fierce Orisha. She is a warrior and fights alongside her husband, Shango. The elders say Oya is so determined, she will wear pants and grow a beard to go to war. She is represented by the wind, storms, hurricanes, tornadoes, and earthquakes. Oya's force can be so severe that she can devastate towns and cities in a matter of minutes. Oya is also known to be owner of the marketplace. This is because of her great speaking and analytical abilities. Children of Oya can be cunning and are especially gifted at winning people over. My aunt in Ocha Mama Ayo, an elder priest of Obatala and well-respected sage of the religion, would always say Oya is one of the most beautiful Orisha ever. She said, "Oya is so beautiful, she must wear a mask because her beauty blinds".

Young priest of Oya, Karla

Oya also represents transitions and change. She is the Orisha you go to when you need to make some serious changes in your life. Many of the elders speak of the relationship between Yemonja and Oya as being contentious. They however, are sisters. When working together, these two orishas can be an unconquerable force. Oya has embraced me many times, and she will help you, as you navigate through life.

THE QUICK HITS—OYA STATS

❖ **Praise:** Heri Hekua Oya de

❖ **Number:** nine

❖ **Colors:** nine different colors, maroon, dark red-brown, burgundy, copper

❖ **Day:** February 2 or October 15

❖ **Special Stuff:** *irukere*, copper, masks, machetes, windmills, pinwheels

❖ **Special Food:** eggplant, chocolate, bean cakes, palm oil

❖ **Domain:** cemetery entrance, rivers, storms

Mi Olokun

I can see clearly now that the rain is gone. I can see all the obstacles in my way.
Gone are the dark clouds that blind me. It's going to be a bright,
bright, sunshiny day."
(Excerpt from "I Can See Clearly Now" by Johnny Nash)

Olokun is the Orisha who resides in the ocean with Yemonja. He is the Orisha for the subconscious, and is often identified with slavery and the Middle Passage because so many Africans lost their lives during the journey from Africa to the Americas. I consider Olokun my savior because this Orisha has opened doors of opportunity for me. Olokun is the Orisha of wealth and hidden treasures. He is also the Orisha of what is not visible to the naked eye. One refrain referring to Olokun is "no one know what lies at the bottom of the sea."

I had Olokun before I made Ocha. I remember bringing Olokun to my off-campus apartment. Initially, I kept Olokun in my bedroom, but I was having too many deep dreams, so my godmother suggested I move him to another room. Olokun was now in my living room, hanging out among all my college friends. Just like with my warriors, nobody messed with my Olokun or even asked questions—he just blended in. And I was grateful because working with my Olokun helped me to keep my sanity. I would take an Olokun bath to cool off when things got too crazy. As matter of fact, Olokun baths were my mother's secret weapon. She would make me go into the bathroom and strip. I stood there bracing for a butt whipping, and here she would come with a basin of cold Olokun water. It usually shocked the stupid out of me, so it was definitely effective.

Olokun is the Orisha that tells us to open our eyes. There are things right in front of us, but we are not seeing them. This could be for good or bad. This Orisha wants you to be able to see clearly—on the physical *and* spiritual tip. Olokun is definitely the Orisha to go to when you are feeling depressed or just not able to pull yourself together. But you can also go to Olokun and ask him to help you with money issues; he will help you out of bleak financial situations.

Young priest of Yemonja, Olori at the Ocean

THE QUICK HITS—OLOKUN STATS

❖ **Praise:** Awani Olokun eh, Awani Olokun eh, ma ting ma ting I eh, ma ting mating I eh

❖ **Number:** seven or four

❖ **Color:** blue

❖ **Special Stuff:** seashells, coins, foreign currency

❖ **Special Food:** molasses, coconut candy

❖ **Domain:** the ocean

MI IBEJI

Ibeji is a Yoruba word that means twins. The Ibeji Orisha are twin Orisha named Taiwo and Kehinde. This Orisha strengthens spiritual growth and development. Usually, many people receive this Orisha on the road to making Ocha. Ibeji are children Orisha. They are often associated with material prosperity; they bring luck and good fortune to your home. In Yoruba tradition, the Ibeji played a significant part in family life; a mother being able to give birth to two children was a great blessing, as it symbolized the continuation of humankind. However, because they are child Orishas, sometimes they are considered mischievous. Whenever you are feeling really down and out, it's a good idea to throw an Ibeji party and invite lots of children. Be sure to have plenty sweets on deck.

The Ibeji dance was one of the first Orisha dances I learned. It's so simple. In most cases, you only sing to Ibeji during an Oro, but it's fun to see everyone fall into step and do the dance trot to Ibeji. Like my warriors and Olokun, I also took Ibeji with me when I went away to college; they're small Orisha in representation, but mighty powerful.

When I received them around twelve or thirteen years of age, I was told that they would help me deal with people's negative energy and draw positive energy to my life.

Also, it's good to have Ibeji energy around you. All of us have been responsible for taking care of little children, whether baby-sitting for others or taking care of little brothers and sisters. Ibeji will help you do a good job with those experiences. Ibeji are the older brother and sister to another Orisha, Idowu. According to the *apataki*, Idowu is Oshun's son after the Ibeji, but she dressed him like a girl so that Shango would not take him from her and give him to Yemonja to raise. Generally, I treat my Idowu very similar to how I treat Ibeji.

My daughters Athena and Itala with their father Nestor after a bembe.

THE QUICK HITS—IBEJI STATS

❖ **Praise:** Ibeji la o mole dun, beji la o mole dun, beji beji la abekun lare

❖ **Numbers:** two, four, seven

❖ **Colors:** red for boy/blue for girl

❖ **Special Stuff:** toys

❖ **Special Food:** candy, bean cakes, chicken and rice

Mi Aganju

Aganju is the Orisha that deals with the heart, emotions, and inner core of one's self. Aganju's domain is the volcano and the river. A volcano is that natural wonder that is always hot, alive, and bubbling just beneath the surface of the earth. There is always the possibility of a volcano erupting, and when it does, its hot, molten lava haphazardly destroys everything it touches. Our prayer is that the volcano never erupts. In this sense, we think of Aganju as having the wisdom and fortitude to maintain control under great pressure, because without it, Aganju knows he could blindly destroy the world.

Because of this aspect, Aganju helps people with emotional instability. Aganju is an Orisha you can go to deal with emotions like uncontrollable anger or rage. Personally, I often say Maferefun (Praise/ blessing to you) Aganju, because I know when I received this Orisha he helped me to not explode when I was infuriated. You'll sometimes hear priests refer to their most heated moments as life before they had Aganju.

Aganju is about change. Aganju is also represented as the ferry-man. He crosses people from one side of the river to the next. He has a very close relationship with Oshun. As Aganju navigates the rivers, Oshun helps to keep him cool. Aganju also has a close relationship with Yemonja.

Many children of Aganju are deep thinkers; they often say things that are insightful, yet at times, they are misunderstood. My mother's twin in Ocha was an Aganju. She had a strong personality, and many people either loved her or feared her. She was extremely knowledgeable about the religion and believed in staying true to your house's traditions. She also possessed tremendous creative talent. The beauty of this woman is that she kept it real. Aganju children are very loyal to their convictions.

Growing up in my *ile*, one of the best moments was to watch my two godbrothers, Baba Charles, ibae and Baba Jay dance to Aganju. They were both tall and skilled dancers. When these two brothers by blood did the Aganju dance, they would take high steps as if they were walking over mountains. Their erect bodies would jump, take huge strides, arms moving in perfect rhythm, as if carrying an *oshe*, clearing the path of all that was in their way. Added to the moment was when their sister, my godsister Mama Joan, who has Shango crowned, would join in the dance. It was always an exciting experience.

THE QUICK HITS—AGANJU STATS

❖ **Praise:** Aganju Shola ki nigbe O

❖ **Also Known As:** the Ferryman

❖ **Number:** nine

❖ **Colors:** deep red, burgundy, green, brown

❖ **Day:** November 16th

❖ **Special Stuff:** *oshe*

❖ **Special Food:** plantains, gofia balls, honey

❖ **Domain:** volcano, river, earth's core, desert, sun, palm tree

MI BABALUAIYE

Babaluaiye is a celebrated Orisha in the African diaspora. He is known as Omolu in Brazil and is often associated with St. Lazarus in Catholicism. His greatest gift to people is that he is a healer; he is the Orisha that deals with sickness, pestilence, and other communicable diseases. Babaluaiye helps clean people of these problems. Often times, people will have a Babaluaiye altar at their front door. It may be represented with a statue of St. Lazarus on crutches with two dogs licking at his wounds. This altar is used to help clean off sickness and unhealthy things as soon as you or someone else enters your home.

Babaluaiye is a royal Orisha. In one of the *apatakis* (Orisha stories) he is dancing on his one leg, and the people start laughing at him. He curses the people with disease and pestilence for ridiculing him. As a result, he is banished from the land. Babaluaiye travels to a different land, where he makes himself king. In his new land, instead of plaguing people, he uses his gifts to heal his loyal followers.

Babaluaiye is also an Orisha of wealth and abundance. He has a special relationship with Shango; they are said to be brothers. The other Orisha that are also very closely connected to Babaluiaye are NanaBuruku, Nanu, and Oxumare. In the United States and Cuba, you don't hear of a person being initiated as a priest of Babaluaiye, but it is pretty common in Brazil.

Babaluaiye Apataki

In old primitive times when the African world was being created, Babaluaiye did not live an organized and proper life. He wanted to live on his own and did not want to obey the older Orishas. He was so disobedient that he caught every contamination that there was in the Yoruba territory. The complaints were so numerous about him that all of the priest gathered together and he was repudiated because of his unhealthy condition. No one offered help or presented him with offerings of any kind. He was subjugated by his sons who saw him as a cripple, walking with a cane. The only Orisha who had pity for him was Elegba. As penalty for his sins, the Yoruba's did not speak to him or hear him. And they sewed up his dillogun (cowrie shell used for Orisha to speak) in an aha (broom), so that he wouldn't be able to express his feelings. Babaluaiye seeing himself rejected by his own people exited himself to another town. When he passed certain tribes they would throw water at him saying Molo bor tu (take the harm with you). In his travels, Babaluaiye met with Esu who took him to the house of Orumila. Orumila told Babaluaiye that he had been left silent because of his disobedience, but that he would be greatly admired in another land. He would have to do an ebo first with different grains and he would always have to be with a dog. Babaluaiye obeyed the advice of Orumila and thanked Esu. When they left, Esu got him a dog from Ogun and Osain. Babaluaiye continued on his way until he reached Dahomey. In Dahomey, the king of the land killed and plundered and did whatever he desired to his people. When Babaluaiye arrived, and the king saw him, the king immediately kneeled before him and asked for his forgiveness for his wrong deeds. For listening to Orumila's advice, Olofi anointed Babaluaiye and cleansed him of his sickness. Babaluaiye became king in Dahomey, and from that point on was respected throughout all of Yoruba land.

THE QUICK HITS—BABALUIYE STATS

❖ **Praise:** Atotoo!

❖ **Also Known As:** Omolu, Asojana, Soponna

❖ **Number:** seventeen

❖ **Colors:** purple, black, brown

❖ **Special Stuff:** crutches, *aha* (broom), burlap

❖ **Special Food:** all ground provisions, coconut water, cactus, sesame candy

❖ **Day:** December 17th

MI ORUNMILA

Ifa is a significant system of divinity that is aligned and closely interconnected with the practice of Orisha worship in the Yoruba tradition. Orunmila is the Orisha of Ifa. He is also known as Orula or Orunla. Orunmila is a herald Orisha and is held in high esteem. He is considered the voice of Oludumare. He has a very close relationship with Elegba. Orunmila is said to know the secrets of Ori (the head) and to know the destiny of people.

During my years I only knew of men to be priests of Ifa. These men are called babalawos. That was the Yoruba (Lucumi style) tradition that had been passed down in my house and is passed down in many *iles* that descend from Cuba. However, in recent years, women are now being initiated into Ifa in Africa. They are called Iyanifas. Unfortunately, the idea of women being initiated to Ifa has caused a lot of controversy in our communities. This is an area where a lot more information needs to be investigated before it can ever really be accepted in the Yoruba Lucumi tradition.

A lot of the Babalawos in the Yoruba Lucumi tradition were actually initiated as priests to a particular Orisha before they went to Ifa. The rule for many years was that when you went to Ifa, you sort of put aside the practice of Orisha and devoted your time to studying in Ifa. This too has caused a lot of stir among Yoruba practitioners; some believe that one should still able to practice in both systems.

People visit babalawos to get consultations on things that are going on in their lives. Although I don't remember getting a reading from a babalawo as a child, I do remember my mother's godfather in Ifa. His name was Padrino Pancho Mora, Ifa Marote, ibae. This man was very significant in many African-Americans lives. According to Baba John Mason, he helped Baba Osergiman establish the Yoruba Temple in Harlem. Pandrino Pancho lived in the Bronx; I remember visiting his home with my mom, on a number of occasions. He had a kind disposition and a handsome face for an elderly Cuban man. I felt at ease in his presence. To this day, his is the first name called in my mojubas mentioning the deceased people in my religious lineage. When I was initiated to Yemonja, my first godfather in Ifa was Baba Renaud Simmons, ibae (Shango Dei/Ifa Alafia). A babalawo and priest of Shango, he was a well-respected Oriate for many years, before he went to Ifa. Many remember him as being charismatic, vocal, and a ladies man (he practiced polygamy), but more importantly he had a reputation for being a superior diviner. When people got a reading from him, they knew it would help their lives. Several years ago, I received Kofa, a special Orisha given to women that derives from Orunmila. The man who gave me this Orisha, Padrino Pablo (EjiOgbe) is now my godfather in Ifa. He is a highly skilled Yoruba Lucumi practitioner from Cuba, who was also initiated as a priest of Elegba before becoming a babalawo.

The babalawo's technique of doing a reading is different from that of a priest of Ocha. The babalowo reads with an *opele* (chain) and an *ikin* (palm nuts), whereas an oriate, italero, or Ocha priest uses *dillogun* (shells) for divination. Their system seem a bit more complex, and their information is often more in-depth on the *odu*.

Most people who are in Ocha have a special relationship with a babalawo. Often they have to receive their warriors from Ifa, or the *illeke (necklace)* and *ide* (bracelet) of Ifa. According to the *apatakis*, the *ide* symbolizes a pact between Orunmila and *iku* (death). When Iku sees the *ide* of Ifa on a person, he is to pass them by if it is not their destined time to die. Thus, through divination, the babalawos play a special role in serving as intermediaries between Orisha, Egun, and other spiritual entities that exist in the world.

ORUNMILA APATAKI (ADAPTATION)

One day John was going to a party. He was walking along the road. Earlier that morning he had read the day and it said that he was not to accept rides from anyone. While he was walking down the street, a guy on a motorcycle came by. The guy recognized the traveler as John. He asked John where he was going. When he discovered they were going to the same place, he offered him a ride on his motorcycle. John considered it since he still was about eight long Brooklyn blocks away, but then he remembered his reading form earlier. John thanked the guy, but told him he was good and that he would just keeping on walking unless the bus came. The guy replied to John, "Okay man, peace out". After traveling a little distance more, the guy on the motorcycle made too sharp a turn when he reached Fulton Street. He flew off his bike, hit the streetlamp, and died on the spot. *If you listen to the advice that is given, it may save your life.*

THE QUICK HITS—ORUNMILA STATS

❖ **Praise:** Ifa moro te, ifa moro te

❖ **Colors:** green and yellow; green and red

❖ **Special Day:** October 4th

❖ **Special Stuff:** *opele, ikin*

❖ **Special Food:** Coconut and yam

CHAPTER IV
GOT OCHA/MAKE OCHA

When my mother made Ocha, her *ita*, which is a lengthy reading divined from particular Orisha, said I had to make Ocha as well. At the time, I was only nine years old. All I thought about then was that they must be crazy because I was not about to walk around bald-headed. Yet, as I grew up, making Ocha was something that was always looming over me. When I got readings it would always come up, or if I attended a *bembe*, Orisha came down and pushed the issue. I recall being at a *bembe* in Flatbush, Brooklyn, and this lady was mounted with Shango. For some reason, I really loved that Orisha. Anyway, Shango followed me around a room and made me salute him, and then he picked me up in the air. Shango went around the room collecting money for me to make Ocha. During another occasion, a woman had Oshun mounted and Oshun did the same thing. During those times there seemed to be a really big push for me to make Ocha.

The years passed, and along the road I received Ibeji and later Olokun, which are usually the first two Orisha you receive on the path to making Ocha. My godmother said that I really needed them to help me spiritually and that they would bring me luck. As I mentioned earlier, when I went off to college, I still hadn't made Ocha, but I did take my warriors and Ibeji with me. Interestingly, my friends at college never paid any attention to the Orisha in my dorm room. My Elegba and Ogun sat by the door, and I swear they must have been invisible to people because honestly no one ever said a thing or asked any questions—they didn't even touch them. However, when I moved off campus, my best friends and roommates, Roni and Sonya, were both curious about the religion. I would tell them things in bits and pieces, for instance about cleaning off with pennies and throwing them in the street, or about not sleeping on dark sheets as it caused bad dreams. Plus, I would inform them about various aspects of different Orisha. From our conversations over the years, I marvel that until this day, Roni proudly thinks she knows more about this religion than any other non-Yoruba person out there.

While I was away at school, my mother was preparing to make my younger sister's Ocha. We were told it was extremely necessary because as a baby my mother had walked onto the throne with her in tow, and that was taboo. You remember that during the first seven days of initiation the new initiate has to stay in a special area of a special room. That area is called the throne and only priests are allowed to go there. If an uninitiated person goes there by accident, it's like they have taken on something that only full initiation will have to settle and it needs to be done right away. Often the Orisha makes it happen in order to begin that person's initiation. So in 1985, my sister, Manny, was initiated to Oshun. She was only nine years old at the time. I was proud of her because she didn't seem to be freaked out about her hair being cut. Perhaps it was because a few years earlier, she and my other little sister Zuwena had their hair shaved off due to a scalp disease. Manny hollered then, but this time she seemed real cool about it. I came to visit her on her throne. At the time, I was dating the rapper Dana Dane. He came to visit her on the throne as well, and said a few rhymes for her. Although he had never been around anything like Ocha before, he seemed very comfortable in the setting. Over the years, I have found it remarkable how easily my friends have adjusted to me being a Yoruba priest. Some of my friends at first thought I was going to change drastically and be some kind of overly pious, reserved person. They were happy to discover that I went through my Iyawo year (the yearlong initiation process to become a priest in the religion) and came out still me. Throughout the years, I have changed though; it's part of growing up and maturing. Yet fundamentally, I am still me. Orisha would not have me be anything other than myself.

My grandmother Ms. Kay and daughter Assata, both priests of Obatala

So why do you have to make Ocha anyway? There could be a number of reasons, but let's explore some of them. One reason why you have to make Ocha is because you need it to save your life. You may be in poor health (sometimes you don't know it), and making Ocha is a big *ebo* that you might have to do to be well. Many adults also make Ocha for health reasons, although sometimes their commitment to Orisha is slightly different than other practitioners. Another reason why some might need to make Ocha at an early age is because they were born as Abiku spirits. In Yoruba, this is a spirit that is born to earth for a short period of time but dies and continues to be rebirthed to the same mother. It is of great anguish to the mother, so to break that pattern, Ocha is made to the child. Another reason why you might need to make Ocha is because you are destined to do great things in the world. An official consecrated ceremony will allow you to be recognized on earth and in the spirit realm as the royal person that you are. Luckily, if you have ocha, you will have Orisa to help you with your many challenges throughout life.

In terms of the children in my family, I think the primary reason we must make Ocha is because of the Ocha lineage that now exists. When my oldest daughter, Assata, made Ocha, she became the fourth generation of Yoruba initiates in my family line. Let me just say this was over a span of thirty years, with my mother having been the first followed by my sister Manny, me, my sister Zu, my grandparents, and then Assata. My niece Folasade, and my next two daughters, Itala and Athena, have since made Ocha, as well. Folasade is connected to Ocha on both sides of her family; her father, Ademola has Oshun crowned, and his mother, Mama Yafe, has Shango crowned. It seems that children who are born into strong family Ocha ties are usually called to make Ocha, not only for their own uplifting but so that they may also be keepers of the tradition. Children should grow up being practitioners of the religion so that it can become an everyday part of them. **You are an important part in carrying on the tradition because you are the future.** If we don't teach you to give sacrifice, praise and honor to Orisha and Egun, who knows, one day they might cease to exist. It is definitely a reciprocal relationship.

Mom with fam: Ademola, Manny and Zuwena, and my nieces Kamira, Masani and Folasade.

THE QUICK HITS—REASONS YOU MUST MAKE OCHA

❖ Your family lineage

❖ Keeper of the Ocha tradition

❖ Save your life

❖ Destined for greatness

Chapter V

Bembe Days

One of the biggest ways in which Yoruba people honor their Orisha is by playing a *bembe* to them. In most cases, people play to a particular Orisha like Shango or Oshun. An elaborate throne is set up and adorned with the colors and different types of foods that the particular Orisha likes. On the day of a *bembe*, people arrive usually wearing all white. At times, some of the priests might have on other colors, especially colors representing their Orisha or colors representing the Orisha that the *bembe* is being played for. The standard norm for *aleyos*, though, is usually to wear white. For women this consists of a white blouse and a mid-length white skirt. Women have a *gele* (head tie) to cover their heads. Men wear a white shirt and white pants, with a *kofi*, (hat), to cover their heads.

Three young priest after a ceremony: Tiffany, Aganju Priest, Shani, Oya Priest, and Adenike, Oshun priest.

When you first get to a *bembe* you should salute the throne and give a *derecho,* a monetary offering. Remember that the throne is where the Orisha itself has been placed and all who attend must go there to establish their presence, to give praise (salute) and to be prayed for by a designated priest. Priests and aleyo salute by prostrating fully before the Orisha. Others just touch the floor and kiss their finger. There will be a decorated basket there for where you put your donation. If you don't have any money, Orisha understands, but if you can sacrifice a dollar or five dollars or more, then you should. After saluting the throne, you then seek out your godparents and salute them. Remember that priests are considered to have the Orisa in their heads and that is why they are saluted. If you don't have a godparent, you should start saluting some of the elder priests in the room. In this situation you aren't necessarily obligated, but you want to be respectful to everyone. Saluting is a great way of showing your respect and humility to the priests and the Orisha they carry. Participating in a *bembe* can be a lot of fun. The priests dance up front closer to the drummers, while the *aleyos* usually dance behind them.

THE QUICK HITS—GOING TO A BEMBE

❖ Cover your head

❖ Wear white

❖ Salute the throne

❖ Practice the songs

❖ Participate in the singing and dancing

❖ Salute the priest older than you in Ocha

❖ Back up some and let priests dance in front of the drums

CHAPTER VI

I GOT PARENTS AND GODPARENTS, TOO!

In most cases, once you receive your *illekes* or an Orisha from a person, they become your godparent. As a godchild to that person, you have an obligation to fulfill—not only to that person who has taken on the responsibility of guiding you and taking care of your spiritual development, but you also have an obligation to their principal Orisha. What I mean is that there are two parts to this relationship you have established for yourself. It is your obligation to nurture the relationship that you have with your godparent(s). It is also your duty to pay respect to their Orisha. Depending on your Ocha house, you might do things differently, but generally, godchildren go and salute their godparents' Ocha on their Ocha birthdays and on the designated special Orisha day. Customarily, godchildren take an offering to the Orisha of one or two coconuts, two candles, and a *derecho*.

In many cases, when you become a godchild, you are not just connected your godparent, but with a string of other people who become your godbrothers or godsisters—some of them might be like your god-aunt or god-cousin, but we usually just call each other godbrother or godsister. It's really all good to have that extended family, but recognize that it does work just like a family. They will be there to help you, teach you new things, and have fun with. They will also be there to get on your nerves and piss you off. It's OK; you'll survive it—that's balance.

Understanding the dynamics in the relationship between a god-parent and a godchild is extremely important. It can determine how much you will learn as an *aleyo* and sometimes how fast you will move on the road to making Ocha. The biggest thing to remember when dealing with your godparent is respect. I am going to emphasize this: *respect*! No matter what the situation, you must remember that your godparent took time from his or her life to take care of you and offer you guidance. The godparent/godchild relationship isn't always easy. There will be times that you will feel as if you are being wronged or neglected. That may lead to you having bad feelings or anger towards your godparent. It happens, sometimes. Work hard to let go of those emotions. In the big picture of things, damaging the relationship with your godparent isn't worth it, and it will cause you more heartache. When these moments arise, either let it go or find a time when you can talk to your godparent about how you feel in a non-accusatory manner. Well pretty much, that's the unpleasant side of things. Most times you will feel that you are lucky and loved to have another caring parent.

Also, it is important that you reach out and communicate with your godparent; the responsibility really does lie with you to do that. Growing up as a child, I had a godfather and a godmother. When it came time to make my Ocha, I was made by my godmother and then got an additional godmother, who is my ojubona. My godfather lived in Africa so he was unable to make my Ocha at that time. However, all of them are very different yet very important to me, and the lessons they bring to my life are invaluable. As I grew up, I found my relationship with my godparents to be a variety of experiences. My godfather was always cool and said things to me like "You know you're my favorite godchild," which I, of course, took to heart and would never let him, my mother, or anyone else forget it. He made the religion seem very cool and natural.

My godmother was very good to me, but she was also serious. She did most of my readings. I used to sit in amazement as she read me and told me things about myself, and was right. I'd sit there and pray that she would be wrong about something. Sometimes, I played dumb like I didn't know what she was talking about, but to no avail. In every one of my readings, I ended up busting out crying like a big baby. You just don't know; I really thought I was too hard for all that, but I actually was a marshmallow when it really came down to getting to the core of me—straight out of do-or-die Bed-Stuy, and crying and snotting all over the mat. My ojubonna was always very kind; her house was where I escaped to when I needed to get away from my mother for a minute.

My relationship with my godparents blossomed over the years because of my mother's very close relationships with them as well. I was always at their house or around for some function. Your parents may have different godparents than you, so you need to always make time to visit them and just be around, especially if they are doing a ceremony.

Here's a quick inside tip for learning a lot of Ocha stuff (even stuff you probably shouldn't know). Sit around when the day is over and get to listening. If you don't know how to listen, quick lesson—shut your mouth, don't make eye contact with anyone, and look as invisible as possible. Even better than sitting around, wash the dishes, clean the table, or sweep the floor—you know, look busy, but still be invisible.

This is how you pick up on some of the most valuable things regarding Ocha, not to mention you'll probably get an earful of juicy gossip as well.

One thing that many of us really need to recognize is that our godparents aren't perfect. They are people with their own lives and experiences, some bumpy, some flawed. They still have bills to pay; they still have to beat the pavement in search of job opportunities, no different than us. But what they do have, and continually strive to attain, is enlightenment. And through this enlightenment they are trying to help us carve out our way in the world. Sometimes you may even wonder how a lawyer can be a good godchild to a godmother who is, say, a hotel clerk? If the godchild is smart, he or she will recognize that it's not all about that—titles of distinction to make you feel more important than someone else. You are on a spiritual journey, and the ego and the arrogance of who you presume you are, needs to be stripped away. You will be a better person when you don't fall victim to American society's status quo. This is not to say that you shouldn't feel fulfilled by the accomplishments you have made in your life—they are yours, and you have a right to be proud. But it is important to not hold your torch, your personal flame, up against another just to see if your light is burning the brightest. **Humility is the key to dealing with your godparents** (and everyone else, too) and not losing yourself perspective in this instance.

When I made Ocha, I remember the Oriate telling me during the *ita* that I could never be friends with my godmother. I was sitting there looking at him screw-faced, thinking, *What are you talking about? My Godmother and I are cool* (even though we had had a big blow-up the week before my Ocha). It was my desire to one day be grown enough that we'd be friends. But as the years passed, I realized it was some of the best advice I received. I know if I had tried to be a friend to my godmother, I'm sure I would not have been able to maintain the proper level of respect. I should never put her on the same playing field as that of a "homegirl" because my mouth is liable to say anything to my girlfriends. Consequently, I am grateful for the message from my ita because today I still have a very stable and nurturing relationship with my godmother.

Yep, keeping and maintaining a healthy relationship with your godparents is a wise thing. Not long ago my best friend Kateria decided to join the religion after having been around it for many years. One of the biggest problems she had was she didn't think she could answer to someone—she was used to being a free spirit—plus the thought of conforming was, like, dumb crazy. Please—she was grown, successful, and a mother; please believe she wasn't trying to be submissive to anyone. Now, after all these years, she realized that something was missing in her life, and the Orisha were calling for her. Kateria now has a godmother and an ojubona (you get an Ojubona during your *illeke* ceremony too, remember?), and she admits it's not so bad. Yes, she has to answer to her godmother and get permission to do certain things in the religion, but somewhere in herself she realized she needed that—she needed to answer to someone(even though it isn't always easy). We all do. I see it like this: life is just a microcosm of the macrocosm—even Orisha and Egun answer to a higher power, Olofi. Every being answers.

CHAPTER VII
SING ORISHA/DANCE ORISHA

In my mother's house, there was always some sort of Ocha function taking place. A large part of these functions resulted in a *bembe* to the Orisha. People came together to sing and dance to celebrate the Orisha. An *oro* is similar, except there usually isn't any dancing. At *bembes* and *oros*, there are specific songs that are sung to each to Orisha. The first Orisha song I learned was a song to Yemonja: "Kai Kai Kai Yemonja alode, Kai Kai Kai Asesu olodo" I vividly remember Mama Wambui, ibae singing it to all the children in the house. We would practice doing the Yemonja dance, holding the edges of our skirts and shuffling our feet side to side like the waves of the ocean or a wind blowing them. From there, it was on to one of Elegba's songs, "Elegba, Elegba, Aso kede kelemeche, Elegba, Elegba, Alaroye kilombo che." We jokingly call them Ocha Songs 101. Another of my earliest recollection of learning Orisha music was with Mama Olufemi, an Obatala priest who was very close to Baba Lloyd and Mama Stephanie. As children, we were not really part of the classes, but we were able to sit around and learn the songs and dances that were being taught to the elders. Later in life, there were no better times than going to one of our house bembes and listening to Mama Ola and Mama Amma singing, and Baba Olukase, ibae, and Baba Neal drumming. At some point, Baba Larry also became a regular drummer in our ile, as well. The majority of the songs and dances to Orisha that I, and thousands of others know, is because of this dynamic group known as *Omiyesa*.

The best thing about Orisha songs and dances is that they don't change. You could go away and not sing them for fifty years, and when you came back, the same song to Obatala will still be getting sung at *bembes*. Why? Because repetition is important. If you are at a *bembe* and you don't know any of the songs, guess what, it's OK. We all started out that way, but the beautiful part is you'll eventually catch on and get it. The first thing you need to do is just practice humming along—listen to the *akpon*, that's the lead singer; then listen to the response from the chorus of people. After a while you'll be able to mumble a few of the lines. It'll take time and some practice before you really get the songs down pat, but hang in there-you'll get it.

Omi Yesa - Mama Amma, Mama Ola, Baba Neil, and Baba Larry

While you are learning the songs, make sure you work on doing some of the dances that go with the songs for different Orisha. Try to master what I call the basic Orisha three-step dance. It isn't hard to learn, and no matter what's going on, folks will always be doing that general step so you'll always look good and in place.

Another thing that will help you to learn the songs is to ask permission if you can record them at a *bembe* and then go home and practice. That might not always be possible, but one good thing is that many of the songs have already been recorded by various artists around the United States and abroad, so there really is no shortage of music. When I'm trying to learn a new song, I literally will play it over and over again; I'll write it down just how it sounds and read from my cheat paper till I feel comfortable enough with knowing the song. Once I master a new song, I look forward to hearing it at a *bembe* to show off my newly learned song skills.

—

CHAPTER VIII
REPRESENT, REPRESENT!

Those who know do not die like those who do not know.

—*Yoruba Proverb*

When I was growing up people would ask me, "What's your religion?" I would quickly pipe up and say, "Yoruba," because deep down, I think I liked being different. It didn't matter to me that they didn't know what I was talking about and that it would always lead into the expected question "What's that?" I loved the option of either engaging them with a basic 101 breakdown on the religion or telling them, "Back up off me—don't worry about it. It's just something my mother's into." It usually depended on who I was talking to and what mood I was in.

In so many ways, our practice of the religion allows us to do that—just blend in with the rest of folks. I tell people all the time that they would never know who is a Yoruba practitioner just by looking at them, although there are some things that give us away. The first clues are probably the Orunmila *ide* you are wearing and then the *illekes*. Being completely dressed in all-white clothes is also another indicator. By the way, we wear white to most of our functions out of respect to Obatala. Also, it's like our uniform, and it's a cool color. It's light, and it reflects energy as opposed to absorbing certain types of energy. Anyway, whenever you wear clean, all-white clothes, it doesn't matter the setting, you always have that crisp, pure look. It makes people feel good to be around you.

Even though growing up I mostly liked being bold in talking about my religious practice, I found that some of my friends did not. It was easier for them to say, "I'm Christian or I'm Muslim," than explain the religion to people who were clueless. It didn't bother me too much to discuss my religion with folks, although I do recall times when my mother would start explaining our religion to Christian family members, I would feel a little awkward and roll my eyes up in my head. My mother never ever wavered in standing up for being a Yoruba. I guess have to admit, I did misrepresent at times. A lot of my internal conflict was trying to decide if I wanted to fit in like everyone else or be seen as a different (or should I say odd) person in the world. But overall, I knew then, and want you to know now, it is really OK to be unique. We should feel good about this religion and what we do. Don't feel as if you have something to hide. Go ahead and represent!

Everyone in this picture grew up in a house of Ocha, and most are initiated priests. From left to right, Sauda, Fabayo, Athena, Mandisa, Kiani, Akissi, and Zuwena.

As I focus on representing, I must digress and explain some things that are slightly confusing in relationship to why we call ourselves Yoruba. Many African-Americans have gotten into spirited discussions with Yoruba people who were born in Nigeria. The Yoruba Nigerians do not understand why we call ourselves Yoruba. Some have been vehement in expressing we are not Yoruba, and that Yoruba is not a religion, but a way of life. Even some Spanish people from Cuba were thrown by African-Americans using the term Yoruba to identify the religion.

Based on conversations I have had with my godfather, and books I've read like George Brandon's *Santeria from Africa to the New World: The Dead Sell Memories*, I will attempt to explain why we call ourselves Yoruba. As I mentioned earlier, the Yoruba tradition was bought to Cuba

145

and other places through slavery. In Cuba, during the late nineteenth century to mid-twentieth century, many enslaved Yoruba were able to practice their religion alongside Catholicism. Added to this is the fact that most of the Africans who came from the Yoruba region came to Cuba toward the end of slavery. This meant that these late arrival Yorubas were not slaves for very long. They still had memory of their practices at home. To preserve their way of life, many Yoruba people from different Orisha/Yoruba villages were able to band together and initiate each other so that their practices would not die out with one group or generation. The Catholic religion was dominant in Cuba, so Yoruba practitioners pretended to worship the saints when they were actually worshiping their Orisha. Over time, a lot of the practices just blended together, so there was less differentiation between the saints and the Orisha. Certain customs, styles of dress, and religious holidays eventually represented the deities in both religions.

When African-Americans got involved in the sixties they saw that the ritual had been steadfastly maintained undercover through slavery and post-slavery. But now, in a land that at least professed freedom of religion, they sought to restore the Africaness of the aesthetics of their practice including its name. They wanted people to be clear that they were practicing an African religion and worshiping African deities. So what was this religion? It was the traditional religion of the Yoruba speaking people of what is now Nigeria. Thus, many shifted from using terms like Santeria (which is Spanish influenced) and started calling themselves Yoruba (the African term). Agreed, there were minor variations in practices that had evolved over the years. But even in Nigeria today there are variations in practices between the Oyo, and the Ife, and the Ekiti and the Egba and the Ijebu. But there are far more similarities. For the Cuban Yoruba, a mixture of priests of all of these different tribes, a common ground was met and they called it

Lucumi. In the end, the actual changes in any of their practices were slight. African Americans are carefully and respectfully removing the cloak carefully laid by the Lucumi as a necessary cover and are finding that Africa is still there. For instance, the special prayers to the Orisha were still Yoruba, and special ceremonial clothes began to look more like African clothes as supposed to Spanish formal dress.

African-Americans' conscious decision to be called "Yoruba" was a testament of respect for the Yoruba people. It was never an impersonation or a symbol of disregard for the indigenous Yoruba people of Nigeria. It was and still is African-Americans' recognition of the historical and cultural connection they had through this religion with the Yoruba people, who brought their way of life across the Atlantic Ocean during the horrific period of slavery and faithfully maintained it.

With that said, it's your religion, so it's OK to claim it.

CHAPTER IX

IWA PELE—GOOD CHARACTER

"I did then what I knew how to do. When I learned better, I did better."
—*Maya Angelou*

Growing up I found there wasn't enough said to me about Iwa Pele—it sounds so simple now, but the meaning was always disguised in other things like "be good," "don't fight with your brothers and sisters," and "respect your elders." Well, here was the problem—I was doing all that. In my opinion, I was being good. Maybe not to the standards of others, but as far I was concerned, heck, I was darn near Saint Theresa.

For one, I wasn't a stick-up kid. I had friends who were. I hadn't shot or stabbed anyone, not really. And I went to school and passed my classes. Secondly, except for Ketema, my brothers and sisters were younger than me. As the oldest girl, my attitude then was that they had better just listen and do what I say. My older brother Ketema was all smart and brawny, but he was no match for my mouth. When he had had enough of it, he would just lash out and pop me in it. Not fair. It wasn't my fault God made me like that. And thirdly, I did respect my elders. I didn't fight, throw things, or curse at them. It just seemed that every time something went down and I was trying to voice my opinion, I was accused of being disrespectful. It wasn't until I had kids that I really understood what this meant. In a nutshell, what my parents meant was like *"please, please, please, Kemba, please, shut your darn mouth"*. During those moments, my opinion wasn't worth a rusty nickel. I get it now. The rebel within created some hard times for me though. I wish I had understood then that my ultimate purpose was to live my life exemplifying Iwa Pele: good character. I now see a lot of this could have been achieved just by being silent. I guess I should have paid more attention to that old saying, "a wise man listens; a fool speaks". Mmmmm..perhaps.

It seems having Iwa Pele is one of the few universal tenets that govern our lives as Yoruba. In trying to understand this, I realize that it is all encompassing, and there are many trials and errors in living it. It's not that you won't mess up, but more importantly, you need to be cognizant of when you mess up, and the consequences of your actions. Awareness is a good place to be. With each problem or situation before me, I had to learn to be introspective. I wanted to—hell who am I kidding, I *did* shout, curse, scream, and kick ass when things weren't going my way, but later, I recognized that this behavior went against the grain of Iwa Pele. It did not matter my perception of what I thought people may have been doing to me; what was more important was how I handled myself in each situation. That was where the line was drawn between good character and acting-a-damn-fool character.

I remember one time in my teens, I was at a store and purchased some stuff, but what I really needed from the store was a bag of ice.

Well, needless to say, after buying ten other things and waiting in line for twenty-five minutes to pay, I had plum forgotten the bag of ice. The ice containers were right by the door, so as I was on my way out, I told my friend to grab a bag. He asked, "Did you pay for it?" I was like "Of course", and we proceeded to head on out the door. But as fate would have it, when you just aren't doing the right thing, a lady stopped us to see the receipt. It didn't take her longer a few seconds to see that the ice wasn't on there. She gave us that lying, stealing asses, once over look. First I rolled my eyes and dished up one of my mean mugs, then my conscience got the better of me, and I looked away from her accusatory face. We quickly handed over the bag of ice saying it was an oversight and walked out of the store. How Embarrassing. Now what on earth made me think to lift a bag of ice? It had cost just a dollar, and I had only spent twenty-seven dollars, with change to spare. It was the inconvenience—that's all. I didn't want to wait in line again. But the question is this: Was I exhibiting Iwa Pele? When did the good character go out the window on this one? When I told my friend the lie about having already paid for the ice? When I tried to steal the bag of ice? When I looked at the lady like she was crazy for having the nerve to stop me over a damn bag of ice? I'd say all of the above. It really didn't matter that it was seemingly a frivolous thing; the act of stealing was wrong. Period. We left the store, and my friend was ticked off that I said I'd paid for the ice. I was embarrassed but tried to shrug it off as nothing, but it bothered me. Sometimes you can convince yourself that bad judgment is no big deal. I had to recognize that under this umbrella of exhibiting Iwa Pele, swiping things just doesn't work.

Having good character is central to everything we do, but I can't say it's always easy. Like with everything, we must put in the practice. I know many people who can be just as nice as sweet potato pie, but as soon as something happens that they don't like, their fangs come out.

It's like they cannot control their actions when they are hot. But what if we could? What if we could remember to act or exhibit Iwa Pele even in times of distress? Even when people make you want to punch them in the face? Would it make you stronger? Would it make you a better person? Why? Those are the things I reflect on when I am facing my greatest challenges. **How you act, and how you react, matter.** It will shape your perception of yourself and how others perceive you. More importantly, you've got to look at the distressing times as teachable moments. Your friends watch, and they learn by your example. Give a good lesson. If you curse and act crazy, they may lose respect for you and even worse, you will give them a license to behave in much the same manner.

I have spent much of my early life being "the great reactor-vator" speaking without thinking, and being quite defensive. It's refreshing for me to see myself now not reacting to stupid stuff. I breathe, hum, and start counting within. I also remove myself from a difficult encounter, be it getting off the phone or walking away. I think I've mastered this about 85 percent; the other 15 is still a work in progress. But really, that is what it's all about—work in progress. Me. You. Everybody.

CHAPTER X

A CONVERSATION WITH TWO YOUNG PRIESTS OF OCHA

Noni

*Oludare with sister, songtress
Amma Whatt*

NONI AND OLUDARE

1. What Ocha did you make and when?

Noni: I made Ocha for Oshun in 1999.

Oludare: When I was fourteen years old, I was crowned to the Orisha Ogun.

2. Do you feel a connection to your Orisha? How so?

Noni: Yes, I feel a strong connection to my Orisha. I feel them. I see their energy manifest in the world.

Oludare: My connection to Orisha was always there. My parents, Iya Amma Oloriwaa Omo Obatala and Baba Canute Bernard Omo Yemonja Ibaye, both raised me around Orisha. I remember on those nights when I was five or six having nightmares like kids do. My mom didn't read me stories; she took me in front of Obatala and cleaned me with his *irukere*. I remember sleeping like a baby after this. I remember being at *bembes*. My mother and father both sang and played *guiros* together around the New York area. This gave me the connection to music with Orisha, which has to be one of my strongest connections. I remember playing with the both of them and learning songs to all the Orisha at a very young age. My parents were very artsy in general. My mother always made Orisha-related art through music and her sewing machine. My father was a gourd maker. He made *oshes* and *shekeres* for so many people in our community in New York and around the nation. Sometimes I go to different people's houses around the city, people I don't even know, and I find some of his gourds sitting by their Orisha. So art keeps me connected with Orisha heavily. I sing, dance, and play drums for Orisha. I play *anya*, *guiro*, *shekere*, bell, and also sing at *anyas* and *guiros*. This keeps me busy studying new songs and finding out new things about Orisha.

A lot of the secrets to Orisha are hidden in the songs. So, by learning the music, I learned a lot early on.

3. What do you do with your Orisha?

Noni: I pray to my Orisha, throw *obi*, sing to them, dance in front of them, give them offerings, and do *ebo*.

Oludare: I pray to my Orisha. This is my main *ebo*. Before I throw *obi* or get a reading, I always like to pray and see what it is that I feel from them. Orisha are living entities that can communicate with you directly. I like to believe that they communicate with me like they do other people. I follow this wisdom, whether it comes from a feeling I get or actual words I may hear. I sing to them and play music to them. One of the things my parents, my godparents, any other elders of mine have always told me was that the simplest *ebos* can be the strongest. A simple glass of water, a song, or a silent prayer has brought me a long way. I find that a lot of the prayers or *ebos* I do with Orisha reflect right back on me. I pray for the things I need, the things I need to do better. So as I pray to them, I affirm that prayer to myself with repetition. As I hear my voice and my thoughts, I am reminding myself as I ask for the help of Orisha.

4. How do you explain your religion to your friends?

Noni: I explain my religion to my friends as an Afro-Cuban religion where I worship God, aspects of God, and energies that exist in the world. I explain the Orisha as messengers of God and tell them that spirituality is a big part of my religion.

Oludare: Ugh. LOL, I usually start with "I am a Yoruba and I worship Orisha." Depending on their interest, I explain what Orisha are and usually feel the tendency to relate it to Christianity, which helps to explain the history of the name "Santeria." I explain how the Orisha were called saints and that the Africans in slavery used syncretism to hide their practices under Christianity. But I also explain to them that I don't have to do that anymore. And in fact, Santeria and Yoruba are one in the same. I just choose to call myself a Yoruba because I never had to call Shango Santa Barbara. So why call myself a Santero? That's usually how the conversation goes.

5. Did your parents insist you make Ocha? Was it a good decision?

Noni: My parents made me make Ocha to save my life. I made Ocha with my father. It was marked that I needed to make Ocha because Orisha had saved me from death, and I needed to do it to continue to live and have good health. It was a great decision. Without it I would not be here.

Oludare: No, they did not. I wanted to make Ocha. It excited me, and I wanted to know Orisha better from a young age. It was never my parents' decision; it was always mine, and I thank them especially my mother, godmother, and Mama Oseye's Obatala (Obatala in total, basically) for giving me the support and ability to make Ocha. Obatala deemed my Ocha to be a community Ocha at my brother Kofi Omo Obatala's Ocha in 2004. This is what gave my family the ability to make my Ocha. So I must give thanks to my community and all priests, friends, and family who supported me in any way, even in prayer.

6. Do you see yourself practicing this religion when you get older?

Noni: Yes I do. I cannot see myself practicing any other religion. Practicing another religion would seem like a betrayal to my Orisha.

Oludare: Yes, it never gets old.

7. What do you think about *bembes* and *centros*?

Noni: I really enjoy *bembes*. In my opinion they are really fun and I love to dance to Orisha music. I don't really mind *centros*. I don't like the smoke, and as a kid I was sort of creeped out by them but I've grown to not be afraid. I'm actually happy now when I receive information from spirits, Egun, and guides. I also feel great after *bembes* and *centros* because I've cleaned off bad energy.

Oludare: *Bembes* I like because of the music, and the anointing that I feel when singing, dancing, and playing drums. *Centros* I like as well because they develop my relationship with Egun.

8. How did it make you feel to make Ocha?

Noni: I remember feeling really good to make Ocha. I had been through a traumatic experience and kept hearing that Oshun and Orisha were here to save me. It made me trust the idea of Ocha. My mom also immersed me in Ocha basically from birth, so my perception of Ocha was always positive.

Oludare: Happy, also aware about life. Making Ocha so young, I actually would say is a large, extremely large responsibility. Orisha is telling you to live your life this way. But as a child, you want to go every which a way. With this said, it takes a lot of discipline and faith to go with *ita*. I had to find the balance between what they were telling me and my own natural inclinations. They don't always match. Making Ocha has allowed me to help others. Now that I have Ocha, I can participate in more ceremonies and get more things done.

9. What is difficult sacrificing a year as an Iyawo? How did your peers and others treat you?

Noni: I don't really remember. I made Ocha when I was three so I have vague memories. I doubt it was difficult because I was so young and because of where I went to school (Little Sun People), where many people knew about Ocha.

Oludare: My peers treated me fine; they respected me, and my religion. It was the teachers and school officials at my high school who were less understanding and stuck in their ways. One of my deans, on my first day of school, forced me to take of my head covering within my three months. This was probably one of the worst days of my life. It was in front of everybody. He was yelling how he didn't care if it was my religion. School rules, school rules, blah, blah, blah. If it had been a yarmulke, he would have kept his mouth all the way shut. This was a lesson to me. I knew from that moment on that I am not protected everywhere I go in the world, and that there will not always be someone there to say, "He is a Iyawo." At my high school I had to teach a lot of people about what I was. There were no Iyawos at Erasmus at the time, so I was the Iyawo. After that day with my counselor, he began to understand that I wasn't just a disobedient Brooklyn boy, but that every day, I would have this head covering on, regardless of school rules. With the help of my principal, assistant principal, and guidance counselor, my dean never bothered me again.

10. Do you see yourself as different from other people your age?

Noni: Yes, I saw myself as different because adults were always telling me I was different. They always said, "You carry a crown on your head," so as I child I had this idea that I was a princess. But then I grew to realize that it was only my religious beliefs that were different.

Oludare: Yes, of course. Other people my age can do whatever and wait for judgment day. I have an *ita*. I can't play those games. I know what is right and wrong and what decisions will be good for me, for the most part. I can't walk blindly; Orisha takes that leisure away. This can feel like both a blessing and a curse, especially as a younger Omolorisha. I also feel safer than the average person. I feel that Orisha makes it clear that death comes when Olofi says so. There is nothing that can deter my life as long as I have faith in Orisha and Olofi. So I feel good with Orisha, and safe.

11. In general, do you tell people that you are Yoruba priest? If so, what do you tell them about the religion—how do you describe it to them?

Noni: I tell people if they ask or if it comes up. It's not really one of my conversation starters. I tell them I'm a priest in a religion that originated in Nigeria but came to the United States from Cuba. I worship deities which represent forces of nature and energy. I usually try to make a comparison of Orisha to Catholic saints or Greek gods so they have more of an understanding. It's easy to explain my beliefs, but not making Ocha. I tell them being Yoruba is a way of life and there's way more to it than the things that are on the Internet. I try to explain that what I do isn't voodoo or black magic because the second you tell people you don't praise Jesus, they question how godly your beliefs are.

Oludare: I do tell people I am a Yoruba priest. Like I stated before, I really wanted to make Ocha and I am happy about the decision I made for my life.

12. What is your relationship like with your godparents, and how do you maintain that relationship?

Noni: I have a good relationship with my godparents. I can talk to them about anything going on in my life. As I get older, it's harder to stay in touch on a consistent basis because I'm busy and they're busy but I see them often. I don't have to make a big effort to maintain a relationship because I see them often to work Ocha.

Oludare: I have a good relationship with my godparents. It takes a lot commitment and outreach to maintain it. We often have busy schedules, so I have to make sure I make myself available to them. I usually have to work around their schedules, but its worth it because if you really want t learn something you have to really want it.

AFTERWORD

Well, there was a glimpse into my story and a few young people's lives of growing up Yoruba. For me, the road has been a roller coaster of experiences. I have pleased folks on my path, yet I have not always lived up to people's expectations. I've done a good job at some things, and done a poor job at other stuff. Yet I remain. Being raised by a pan-Africanist baba and an Ocha loyalist mother was not an easy road. My heart pained on many occasions because this path to adulthood seemed too much and I craved for normalcy in my home life. My sub-consciousness mantra had to be: *Can't we please be regular for just a little while.* Funny though, as I harangue on my uniquely challenged life in Bed-Stuy, I can not forget the easy simple times I did experience at my grandparents home in the Bronx. Looking back, I now know that my mother and baba were giving me a well-rounded childhood by keeping the right family in my life. My grandparents provided a warm sense of old fashioned nurture that was not always present in my Brooklyn home. Both of them would later make Ocha to become priests in the religion. While my grandfather died as a Iyawo from cancer, my grandmother, who is in her eighties now, remains heavily involved in the Obatala Egbe and in many of the functions that take place in our Ocha house. Having multi-generations of family with Ocha is becoming more prevalent in our communities today. Many people are getting their children, grandchildren, and other family members initiated into Ocha. One of the beauties in practicing this tradition is seeing how it is embraced and celebrated in the lives of people who grew up in the religion like me. In the iles, there are artists whose artworks are inspired by Orisha. There are also writers who have created children's books and prayer books to the Orisha. There is a multitude of talented people who have learned beadwork, sewing, and cooking for the Orisha. Others have become master dancers and singers honoring the religion. One of my godsisters is working on her dissertation, which is influenced by the religion. Several of my godbrothers have studied and are now Oriates (officially recognized masters of the rituals) in the religion. A few others have formed organizations dedicated to the continuation and upliftment of the Yoruba religion. And a number of people have taught classes and given lectures on the aesthetics of this religion.

Loving Orisha and this religion is something you have to come into on your own. It's a great space. For me it was about opening my mind to understanding the religion in the context of the experiences of my youth. Everybody's story is unique to them; as you study more and build your relationship with your godparents, your experiences will be special to you, too. Stay steady on your path. This book is only a snapshot to learning about Yoruba Lucumi practice.. There is still so much to know and learn; I've only presented a little bit of information. The best tool for learning is to be present in the doing! Go to your godparents and ask questions; participate in ceremonies and be involved. You will learn more about the religion by doing than by reading any book. It hasn't always been easy, but it sure is beautiful. With the power of Oludumare, Egun, and Orisha in your life, things will fall in place. May you continue on your journey of enlightenment, and do it up good!

GLOSSARY

Abuelo: Grandfather

Akpon: Lead singer at a drumming or other performance

Aleyo: People in the religion who have not gone through the year-long initiation to become an orisha priest. Illeos have usually received illekes and maybe their warriors.

Anya: a special type of *bembe* performed for the orisha

Apataki: story or legend in Yoruba history passed down through oral tradition

Astera: a straw, beach-style mat used for saluting, or sitting orisha on

Baba: father; respect title used when addressing men; title also used for male orisha

Babalowo: a priest of Ifa

Bembe: Drumming, singing, and dancing paying homage to the orisha

Centro: small gathering of mediums to offer prayers to specific ancestors and receive information from spirits

Derecho: Money offering

Dobale: To prostrate before an orisha shrine or a person who is initiated to a particular orisha

Ebo: an offering to orisha or Egun

Efun: lime chalk; Chalky white substance used in many ceremonies for protective or healing purposes

Egbe: society. Special organizations formed with initiated members that represent a particular orisha

Egun: 1. ancestors, deceased people. 2. spiritual guides belonging to a particular person 3. An Orisha

Egungun: a masquerade that appears publicly on specific occasions and dances with an entourage of drummers and singers all around the town. The masquerade connects the entire community to the world of the dead

Gele: scarf or headtie worn by women

Guiro: type of drums used in bembes - not bata

Ibae: term used to refer to a deceased person

Ide: a bracelet representing a particular Orisha

Iku: death

Ile: house; also referred to the community of people who share the same godparent(s).

Illekes (coyales): necklace beads worn for protection. Each is a different color or pattern and represents an orisha. Receiving your *illekes* is the first step in being initiated in the religion.

Irukere: fly whisk usually made of white or black horse hair. Carried by several orisha including Obatala and Oya.

Ita: a lengthy reading (divining) one receives on the third day of their initiation; a reading done after receiving a particular orisha.

Iwe Pele: good character

Iya: mother ; title used when addressing women, especially with priests; title used for female orisha

Iyawo: a person going through the initiation period. Depending on the ceremony, the person could be an Iyawo for a day (receiving *ilekes* or something in Ocha), or for a year (making Ocha).

Kofi: hat worn by men

Madrina: Godmother

Mojubas: prayers asking for praise to God, Egun, and the orisha

Mounted: a person experiencing the possession of orisha

Obi: a coconut used for divination

Obobera: a table dedicated to praying to the ancestors, containing glasses with water, lit candles, spiritual books, pictures, and other effects

Ocha: 1. a ceremony that makes a person a full initiate of the Yoruba religion. 2. a general name used to refer to all orisha

Olofi: God

Ojubona: a person who serves as a second godparent

Olodumare: God

Omolorisa: initiated priest

Oriate: a priest that is ordained to be the officiator of Orisha ceremonies

Orisha (also spelled orisa): Deities that are worshiped in the Yoruba religion; considered God's helpers, as they are reflected in all the elements of earth

Ide– bracelet representing a particular orisha

Oro: a drumming similar to a *bembe* except it is shorter and there is usually no dancing

Oshe: a single- or double-headed axe carried by several orisha including Shango and Aganju

Padrino: Godfather

Santera/Santero: a person who has been fully initiated in the religion

Shekere: handheld beaded gourd instrument that is played at *bembes* and other performances

SOME BOOKS IN
MY PERSONAL LIBRARY

Michelle Bodden: *Obara and the Merchants*. This is a children's book. It is a nice *apataki* story with beautiful illustrations. Ms. Bodden is a priest of Yemonja and an educator.

George Brandon: *Santeria from Africa to the New World: The Dead Sell Memories*. This a scholarly textbook. This book will give you the history of the Yoruba, the slavery experience, and the Yoruba religion coming from Cuba to the United States.

David Brown: Santeria Enthroned. This is a great book that also gives the history of Africans, and a lot of illustrations of the Santeria-Yoruba Lucumi religion.

Mary Curry: *Making the Gods in New York: The Yoruba Religion in the African-American Community* (a dissertation book). This is another tool for learning the history of the Yoruba religion, as well, as understandings of how a house of Ocha in Brooklyn functions. Dr. Curry, ibae, was a priest of Yemonja.

John Mason: *Four New World Yoruba Rituals*. This is a great book on Orisha practice. In our *ile*, this book was a recommended read for new people entering the religion. Mr. Mason is a priest of Obatala, a noted scholar, and a lecturer on the Yoruba religion.

John Mason and Gary Edwards, *Black Gods: Orisa Studies in the New World.* This too is a great introductory book about the Orisha and the religion

John Mason. Araaraara: Wondrous Inhabitor of Thunder. This book is all about the history of Shango.

Ayoka Wiles Quinones, *I Hear Olofi's Song.* This is a beautiful prayer book for the Orisha. Ms. Wiles is a priest of Obatala.

Iyanla Vanzant, *Acts of Faith.* This is a must have when sitting at a *centro.* We use this book often in our daily spiritual rituals, as well. Ms. Vanzant is an Obatala priest and a motivational speaker. She has published numerous self-awareness books.

Marta Vega, *Altar of My Soul.* This a personal memoir style book of Dr. Vega's experience in joining the Yoruba Lucumi community. Dr. Vega is founder of the Caribbean Cultural Center in New York City.

Lloyd Weaver and Olurunmi Egbelade, *Yemonja Maternal Divinity.* This book gives great *apataki* stories on Yemonja and all the other Orisha Yemonja interacts with. Mr. Weaver, a priest of Yemonja, is the founder of Ile Ase, the largest African-American house in America.

There are plenty more good books and reputable authors on the Yoruba religion. These are just some of the few that I own. Because I was raised as a hands-on practitioner of the religion, I did not grow up reading a lot of books on the tradition, plus you had to careful about what you were reading. Fortunately, times have changed to some degree, and there is some good stuff out there, but for practice sake, it's usually a good idea to get the opinion of your godparents or elders in your Ocha house before jumping into all sorts of books on the religion. Additionally, if you still want to learn and experience more in the Yoruba-Lucumi religion, think about participating in a few of these wonderful annual events; they have been around for a number of years and are still going strong.

❖ The Egbe Iwa Odo Kunrin & Egbe Iwa Odo Binrin Rites of Passage Program

❖ The Egbe Omo Obatala International Orisa Conference (usually held the last week in October)

❖ The Yemonja Festival at the Beach (early September, Rockaway Beach, Brooklyn, NY)

❖ Ijo Orisa Yoruba Church (usually every other week in Harlem, NY)

Acknowledgements

Giving thanks to my mother, Mama Oseye Mchawi for your love and support. All praises due to you for bringing this religion to our family and the community, making it stick, and continuing to be a mountain in this tradition and my life. Thanks to my baba, Baba Basir Mchawi, for being a knowledgeable and righteous guiding light in my life throughout all these years. Thanks to Ms. Gloria K. Cooley and the late Mr. James Cooley - the best grandparents! You are a walking example of all that is good and beautiful in the world. A tremendous thanks to my godfather, Baba Lloyd Weaver, for your love over the years, and for your support and invaluable assistance in writing this book. Thanks to my ojubona, Mama Monique Robinson for your undying love for me displayed over and over again, and in being a co-teacher in bringing Yoruba Lucumi practice to my understanding. To my sisters, Zuwena Mchawi Smith, Mandisa Mchawi-Thank God for being in my life-never would have made it without you. To my sister Abena Hill, thanks for your love and beautiful presence in my life. To Alex Spencer, Jr., thanks for always *always* making me do the right thing. To my longtime friend Kateria Niambi, thanks for a whole lot of memories, advice, and just about everything in the many years strong together. To Baba John Mason, thanks and much gratitude to you for your long discussions on the religion, and sharing the knowledge. To Sauda Smith, thanks for helping me understand some of Yoruba language. To Criscilla Stafford, a sincere thanks and appreciation for sharing your pictures with me, and thanks to Marva Martin and Rashid Hill for your invaluable digital graphics assistance. To Noni Abdur-Razzaq and Oludare Bernard, thank you so much for sharing your valuable experiences in growing up in this tradition. To Mama Mtaminika Beatty, my big godsister, thanks for your continued and unwavering support and love of the girls and me. To Salima Moyo Smith, Cuz Yvette Aiken, Shanta Pickett, Adunni Williams, Joan Morgan, and Zahara Duncan, thank you sisterfriends– you make this religion more beautiful everyday. To the Gucci Girl Crew: Cuz Yolanda Sessoms-Jones, Cuz Fahja Bey, Veronica Hawkins, Sonya Smith, Vanessa Henderson, Dawn Jones, Eileen Stokes, Marie Reynolds, Allison Timmonds, Tamelia Hinson, Tracey Allen-Merrill, and Renee Washington – thank you for being my friends for life. To Desmond Carter, my "brother from another mother", thanks for never faltering and always encouraging me to write it out. Thanks to my goddaughter, Victoria Rhames, and my Yemonja sister friend, Sherekaa Osorio, for your much needed editing assistance. And to all my godchildren, Dejon Wallace, Paul Killings, Monica Slade, Dafina Oronde, Cheryl White, and Jason McMichael- I am honored to be and have been your godmother. To my own in-house literary mother, Dr. Kokavah Zauditu-Selassie, thanks for always bugging me about writing, and to my literary, Uhuru Sasa brother, Baye McNeil, thanks for also inspiring me to write. To Lumumba Bandele, thanks for your many years of friendship. To my Atlanta Yoruba Lucumi crew: Senemeh & Seshaut Burke, Maria Fundura, Valentin Martinez, Sharon Rowland, Iya Frances and Baba Femi Humphries, Tracey and Assim Shadee, Baba Reginald Brown, Modupe McIntosh, Afrikiti Parks, Sauda Jackson, and Cheryl Johnson, thanks for your continued love and support over the last twelve years. Also to Wil & Tammie Ozier- a special thanks for your friendship, support, free rides, and encouragement throughout the years, and also your willingness to share your time, books, and knowledge with me. Thanks to Latoya & Elton Fonville, and their daughters Odoyemi and Folade (Camp Kemba's girls), for being my much needed Atlanta family over this last decade. Thanks to the Egbe Inu and Akekos, past and present, of the Egbe Iwa Odo Kunrin & Egbe Iwa Odo Binrin Rites of Passage Program. Much love and appreciation to the beautiful sisters in The Daughters of Isis Book Club, and to the great writers/friends in my City Chapters Writing Group. Thanks to Karen Quinones Miller for imparting your expertise and guidance on our little writing crew. Thanks to Padrino Junior Bermudez, and Gregory Harrison for your continued support of my godmother, mother and Ocha house. Thanks to my friend Joseph K. Kyiamah for being a sage and positive catalyst for change in my life. Thanks to all the mamas who were relentless in growing me up right in this religion: Mama Wambui Smith, ibae, Mama Naima Champ, Mama Joan Robinson, Mama Judith Brabham, Mama Carolyn Jones, Mama Barbara Britton, Mama Shona Sloan, Mama Isyla Barksdale, Mama Cheryl Lawrence, Mama Andrea Battle, Mama Isoke Nia, Mama Akilah Mashariki, Mama Roxanne Perinchief, Mama Fela Barclift, Mama Gail Baptiste, and Mama Bettie Davie. I am also especially thankful for having the best godbrothers and godsisters in the world belonging to Ile Ase, straight out of Brooklyn, NYC.

Finally, finally, finally – A very special thanks to my godmother, Mama Stephanie Thomas Weaver, who has continuously shown me the ways to live with respect and dignity, and continues to teach me about this religion and about life. Thank you Godmother for pushing me repeatedly to write. Heartfelt thanks to you for being the best mentor and teacher over the course of three decades, a goddaughter could ever have. I am blessed.

Peace.
Today, a new day.
Kemba

CHRONOLOGY
OF
159

INITIATIONS
IN THE
HOUSE OF
OLOSUNMI & OKE
SANDE

COURTESY OF MAMA JUDITH AND
MAMA CAROLYN

(SOME NAMES HAVE BEEN DELETED AT THE
PERSON'S REQUEST)

ODUN ORI JOKO	OLORISHA	OCHA NAME	OMO DE	BABA/IYALORISHA	OJU EBONA-KAN
03/31/73	LLOYD	OLOSUNMI	YEMOJA/OGUN	SHANGO GUMI	EFUN DEI
07/02/74	STEPHANIE	OKE SANDE	OBATALA/YEMOJA	ALABUMI	OSHUN MI
1) 07/24/76	OSEYE	ORISAIYE	OBATALA/OSHUN	OLOSUNMI	SHANGO GUMI
2) 07/24/76	IRENE	ADE SHOLA	AGANJU/YEMOJA	OLOSUNMI	OMI DURO
3) 07/30/77	RICHARD	OKANTORUN	OSHUN/OBATALA	OLOSUNMI	OCHA BI
4) 10/15/77	ANDRES	ARIBODE	SHANGO/OSHUN	OKE SANDE	ALABUMI
5) 12/21/77	MARY	OLAMIDE	YEMOJA/SHANGO	OLOSUNMI	ORISAIYE
6) 06/24/78	MONIQUE	OLOSHUNDE	OSHUN/OBALUAIYE	OLOSUNMI	OCHA BI
7) 08/05/78	JACKIE	OLODOBI	OSHUN/AGANJU	ORISAIYE	OLOSUNMI
8) 01/27/79	M'TAMANIKA	OSHUN FUNMI	OSHUN/SHANGO	OKE SANDE	ORISAIYE
9) 05/26/79	JOE T.	OBA KANLA	AGANJU/YEMOJA	OLOSUNMI	IYA GUERRA
10) 06/16/79	MARY	ORU OBA	OBATALA/OSHUN	OLOSUNMI	SHANGO GUMI
11) 08/25/79	GERALDINE	SHANGO FUNMILAYO	SHANGO/YEMOJA	OLOSUNMI	ADE SHOLA
12) 01/05/80	WASCHEERA	OBA DINA	SHANGO/OSHUN	OKE SANDE	ADE SHOLA
13) 02/16/80	CHARLES	SHOLA REMI	AGANJU/OSHUN	OLOSUNMI	OMI TOKI
14) 12/06/80	NAIMA	OSHUN ATILEWA	OSHUN/OGUN	OLOSUNMI	OKE SANDE

15) 01/24/81	JONATHAN	SHOLA IRAWO	AGANJU/OBA	OLOSUNMI	OKE SANDE
16) 01/24/81	JOAN	OMO OGUN LABI	SHANGO/OBA	OKE SANDE	ORISAIYE
17) 02/21/81	WAMBUI	ADELETI	OSHUN/AGANJU	ORISAIYE	OKE SANDE
18) 08/08/81	CAROLYN	OSA YEMISI	OBATALA/OSHOOSI	OLOSUNMI	OKE SANDE
19) 01/09/82	TONI	ADE OKE	OBATALA/OBATALA	ADE SHOLA	OLOSUNMI
20) 02/06/82	BARBARA	OLODOMI	OSHUN/OBATALA	OKE SANDE	OLOSHUNDE
21) 02/13/82	SOJOURNER	OMI RE'LEKUN	YEMOJA/SHANGO	ADE SHOLA	ORISAIYE
22) 03/06/82	ALICE	OMI L'ADE	YEMOJA/SHANGO	ORISAIYE	OLOSHUNDE
23) 05/20/83	YVETTE	ODU BI	OBATALA/OSHUN	OKE SANDE	OSHUN FUNMI
24) 06/02/84	AKISSI	EGUIN KOIDE	OBATALA/OSHUN	OKE SANDE	SHANGO FUNMILAYO
25) 08/18/84	JUDITH	SALAKO	OBATALA/OSHUN	OKE SANDE	OLODOMI
26) 10/ 06/84	MICHELE	OMI KEMI	YEMOJA/AGANJU	ORISAIYE	ADELETI
27) 01/19/85	KIANI	OSHUN APPOLLOJE	OSHUN/OBATALA	OKE SANDE	ORISAIYE
28) 07/13/85	SHONA	SHANGO NI OHUN	SHANGO/YEGWA	OKE SANDE	EGUIN BI
29) 07/20/85	RAYMOND	OMI LOKE	YEMOJA/OBATALA	SHOLA REMI	OLOSUNMI
30) 11/09/85	MANDISA	OSHUN MOREMI	OSHUN/OBATALA	OLOSUNMI	ADELETI
31) 11/08/86	JONATHAN	OMI KANLE	YEMOJA/OBATALA	OKE SANDE	OKANTORUN
32) 06/04/88	CAROL ANN	OMI DINA	YEMOJA/SHANGO	OLOSUNMI	OLOSHUNDE

181

33) 07/09/88	LESLIE	OSHUN ADEBUNMI	OSHUN/OBALUAIYE	ORISAIYE	OSHUN FUNMI
34) 08/26/89	NTOZAKE	ADE SHOKAN	AGANJU/OSHUN	OKE SANDE	SHANGO NI OHUN
35) 08/26/89	ROXANNE	ADENIYE	OSHUN/SHANGO	OKE SANDE	OSHUN ATILEWA
36) 10/28/89	JOSEPHINE	OLOJU-MI LAYE	YEMOJA/AGANJU	ADE SHOLA	OKANTORUN
37) 11/11/89	DENISE	SHANGO GUMI	SHANGO/OBATALA	ORISAIYE	OSA YEMISI
38) 11/25/89	ANDREA	ODU ALA	OBATALA/OSHUN	ORISAIYE	ADELETI
39) 03/24/90	KEMBA	OMI LETI	YEMOJA/SHANGO	OKE SANDE	OLOSHUNDE
40) 04/07/90	MAKEDA	IGBIN LETI	OBATALA/OYA	ORISAIYE	ADELETI
41) 04/07/90	NEFERTITI	IYA TOKUN	YEMOJA/OSHOOSI	ORISAIYE	OSHUN ATILEWA
42) 12/08/90	LEONARD	SHANGO DARA	SHANGO/OSHUN	OLAMIDE	OLOSUNMI
43) 12/15/90	BETTIE	OKANIGBE	ELEGBA/YEMOJA	OLOSUNMI	OKE SANDE
44) 12/15/90	FABAYO	OSHUN KAYODE	OSHUN/ELEGBA	OLOSUNMI	ORISAIYE
45) 02/02/91	MIRIAM	OMI TOLA	YEMOJA/OBATALA	SHOLA REMI	OMO OGUN LABI
46) 06/01/91	ISOKE	OYA NIYI	OYA/SHANGO	ORISAIYE	ADELETI
47) 06/08/91	LYNETTE	OBA NI T'OLA	OBATALA/OBATALA	ORISAIYE	OMI KEMI
48) 06/08/91	ALEX	OBA NI L'AYE	SHANGO/YEMOJA	ORISAIYE	SHANGO GUMI

49)	06/19/92	TYRON	SHANGO ALA TIKU	SHANGO/YEMOJA	OMI L'ADE	ORISAIYE
50)	07/17/92	SHASHALA	OBA DE MEJI	SHANGO/OYA	SHANGO NI OHUN	OKE SANDE
51)	10/10/92	GARY	ORI YOMI	OBATALA/OYA	ORISAIYE	OKANTORUN
52)	10/10/92	ANASA	ABEGUNDE	YEMOJA/OBALUAYE	ORISAIYE	OMI KEMI
53)	05/08/93	ISYLA	ENI OSHUN	OSHUN/SHANGO	OKE SANDE	ADE NIYE
54)	05/29/93	CONRAD	BABA 'SHEGUN	OBATALA/OSHUN	ORISAIYE	OLAMIDE
55)	08/ 6/93	AKILAH	OBA ILU	SHANGO/YEMOJA	ORISAIYE	SHANGO FUNMILAYO
56)	08/13/93	ONAJE	ESHU ADE LORO	ELEGBA/YEMOJA	ORISAIYE	SHANGO WOLE
57)	09/03/93	MICHELE	OSHUN TEMI D'AYO	OSHUN/SHANGO	OLOSHUNDE	OCHA BI
58)	09/11/93	JEAN	SHANGO FO SHALADE	SHANGO/YEMOJA	OMI L'ADE	SHANGO WOLE
59)	01/15/94	ADEMOLA	OYEYE MI	OSHUN/SHANGO	ORISAIYE	OBA NI T'OLA
60)	04/23/94	AYANNA	ABEBE OYIN L'ADE	OSHUN/ORISHA OKO	OSHUN FUNMI	OKE SANDE
61)	06/17/94	SHARON	ADE K'OLA	SHANGO/YEMOJA	ADE SHOLA	OBA NI T'OLA
62)	06/25/94	XXXXXXX	ALA L'ADE	OBATALA/YEMOJA	ORISAIYE	ADELETI
63)	07/28/94	SADIQUA	OBA BINA	AGANJU/OSHUN	SHANGO NI OHUN	EGUIN BI
64)	10/29/94	ZAHARA	OSHUN KO L'ADE	OSHUN/SHANGO	OKE SANDE	OSA YEMISI
65)	11/19/94	SENEMEH	OSHUN FERAN MI 'KAN	OSHUN/OBATALA	OBA NI T'OLA	ORISAIYE

66) 04/ 8/95	PEARL	OSHUN AINA	OSHUN/OBATALA	OKE SANDE	ADELETI
67) 04/21/95	ROBERTO	SHANGO AKIKITAN	SHANGO/OSHUN	ORISAIYE	OMI L'ADE
68) 05/13/95	CHERYL	IRIN T'OLA	OGUN/YEMOJA	OKE SANDE	ORISAIYE
69) 06/10/95	KAMAU	OSIKA	ELEGBA/YEMOJA	OKE SANDE	OMO OGUN L'ABI
70) 10/13/95	DELORES	OSA UNKO	OBATALA/AGANJU	ORISAIYE	OSHUN ATILEWA
71) 01/06/96	JOAN	OKUN S'ADE	YEMOJA/OBATALA	SALAKO	OKE SANDE
72) 02/15/96	ALLEN	SHANGO AKIN TEMI	SHANGO/YEMOJA	SHANGO NI OHUN	BABA 'SHEGUN
73) 03/16/96	ZUWENA	OMI FUNMI L'AYE	YEMOJA/OBATALA	OSHUN ATILEWA	OKE SANDE
74) 04/13/96	URAYOANA	OBA T'ILE FUN	SHANGO/YEMOJA	ADE SHOLA	OMI YALE
75) 04/27/96	SESHAUT	OYA TOKUN'BO	OYA/OBATALA	ORISAIYE	OSA YEMISI
76) 05/18/96	LISA	ERIN T'OMI	OBATALA/OYA	OBA NI T'OLA	OMI L'ADE
77) 05/18/96	SAUDA	OMI DURO	YEMOJA/OBATALA	ORISAIYE	OSHUN MOREMI
78) 06/22/96	FRANKLIN	OLOMI ADE	YEMOJA/AGANJU	SHANGO NI OHUN	OBA BINA
79) 02/14/97	XXXXXX	XXXXXXXXX	YEMOJA/OBATALA	ORISAIYE	OBA NI L'AYE
80) 05/02/97	GLORIA	EGUIN-BI	OBATALA/OYA	ADE L'ETI	OKE SANDE
81) 05/02/97	JAMES	OSHUN YEMI	OSHUN/SHANGO	ADE L'ETI	ORISAIYE

82)	05/23/97	GAIL	EWU ARERE	AGANJU/OSHUN	OLAMIDE	ORISAIYE
83)	06/21/97	MALIK	ESHU ADE WA	ELEGBA/YEMOJA	OKE SANDE	ENI OSHUN
84)	06/24/97	MILAGROS	ABEBE L'OSHUN 'GUNA	OSHUN/OGUN	ORISAIYE	IRIN T'OLA
85)	04/10/98	ASSATA	ORUN MI ADE	OBATALA/OSHUN	OBA NI L'AYE	ORISAIYE
86)	06/26/98	CHANYE	OGUN L'ODA	OGUN/OSHUN	OMI L'ADE	ADEBUNMI
87)	08/01/98	TREVOR	ODO L'AYE	OSHUN/OBATALA	OLAMIDE	OKANTORUN
88)	12/12/98	KOKAHVAH	OKE L'OLA	OBATALA/OBATALA	ORISAIYE	OYA T'OKUN BO
89)	01/02/99	DAVID	ESHU L'ONA	ELEGBA/OBA	ADE SHOLA	ADE K'OLA
90)	01/16/99	OLA	OBA DINA	SHANGO/OSHUN	SHANGO GUMI	ORISAYE
91)	03/19/99	CARLENE	OSHA LO PE-MI	OBATALA/OSHUN	SALAKO	OLODOMI
92)	04/1/99	AJAMU	ALADARE	OBATALA/YEMOJA	ADE LETI	ORISAYE
93)	04/30/99	DEBORAH	OBA FUN MI L' AYE	OBATALA/YEMOJA	ADE SHOLA	OLOJU-MI L'AYE
94)	05/15/99	JOYCE	ORISHANMI	OBATALA/OSHUN	OKE SANDE	OMI L'ERI
95)	07/11/99	TERENCE	ABEBE L'ONA	OSHUN/SHANGO	OLAMIDE	OMI L'ADE
96)	08/20/99	MODUPEOLA	ESHU L'ADE	ELEGBA/YEMOJA	SHANGO NI OHUN	OMI L'ERI
97)	09/04/99	HASSAN	ADE L'OKUN	YEMOJA/SHANGO	ADE NIYE	OSHUN ATILEWA
98)	09/04/99	KAI	ODO 'SHEGUN	OSHUN/OBATALA	ADE NIYE	OKE SANDE
99)	09/10/99	MARIE	OLA MI ODO	OSHUN/ELEGBA	OKUN AINA	ORISAIYE

100) 10/02/99	MALIK	ESHU SHEGUN	ELEGBA/OSHUN	OKE SANDE	ESHU MI WA
101) 10/02/99	NONI	AKWETE OSHUN	OSHUN/AGANJU	OKE SANDE	OSHUN KAYODE
102) 10/16/99	XXXXXXX	XXXXXXXXXX	SHANGO/YEMOJA	ADE SHOLA	OKANIGBE
103) 10/23/99	SHANI	OYA N'ILE	OYA/SHANGO	ADE LETI	OYA NIYI
104) 11/06/99	HERU	OSHA BI OWO	YEMOJA/SHANGO	OMI L'ADE	SHANGO GUMI
105) 03/18/00	RAQUEL	ALA FUN MI PELE	OBATALA/OSHUN	OBA NI L'AYE	SHANGO GUMI
106) 07/07/00	JUDE	EFUN L'OKE	OBATALA/OYA	ORISAIYE	ABEBE OSHUN
107) 07/09/00	COLLEEN	EBUN L'AYE	OSHUN/OGUN	ORISAIYE	OYA T'OKUN BO
108) 11/04/00	ALEJANDRO	ESHU GBEMI	ESHU/YEMOJA	OKE SANDE	ESHU ADE WA
109) 11/30/00	NABINTU	XXXXXXX	OBATALA	OMI L'ADE	OLOJU-MI L'AYE
110) 11/30/00	D. S.	XXXXXXX	AGANJU	OMI L'ADE	OBA BINA
111) 05/05/01	NAIYAH	ODO BI AYO	OSHUN/ELEGBA	ORISAIYE	OYA NIYI
112) 05/19/01	REBECCA	ESHU 'LUGBON DE	ELEGBA/OBA	SALAKO	OKANIGBE
113) 02/17/02	MILANI	OSHUN L'ADE	OSHUN/OBATALA	ORISAIYE	OSHUN MOREMI
114) 05/25/02	DWANA	OLAMIDE	YEMOJA/OBATALA	ORISAIYE	OSHUN ATILEWA
115) 06/15/02	ADENIKE	ODO L'EFUN	OSHUN/OBATALA	OSHUN MOREMI	ORISAIYE
116) 08/24/02	AKIN L'ADE	EFUN S'ADE	OBATALA/YEMOJA	ESU ADE WA	OKE SANDE

117) 03/01/03 WHITNEY	IWA TORUN	OBATALA/OBATALA	ORISAIYE	OYA NIYI
118) 03/18/03 DAFINA	OMIFUNKE	YEMOJA/OBATALA	ORISAIYE	OMI LETI
119) 03/18/03 KAMAU	OSHUN ASODAYO	OSHUN/ELEGBA	ORISAIYE	IBU OKANLA
120) 03/22/03 XXXXXXX.	XXXXXXXXX	OSOOSI/OSHUN	OKE SANDE	OKANIGBE
121) 06/13/03 MICHELLE	SANGO ADE T'EMI	SANGO/YEMOJA	OKE SANDE	OMI L'ERI
122) 07/11/03 XAVIERA	IGBIN SEGUN	OBATALA/YEMOJA	OBA NI L'AYE	OSHUN KO L'ADE
123) 07/18/03 GENEVIEVE	SHANGO SINA	SANGO/YEMOJA	OKANIGBE	OKE SANDE
124) 11/06/04 LEONORA	AFEFE L'OKE	OBATALA/OYA	OBA NI L'AYE	OSHUN APPOLLOJE
125) 11/29/04 LUMUMBA	OPA BAMISE	OBATALA/OYA	ORISAIYE	OYA NIYI
126) 04/17/04 KALILA	OMI FEMI	YEMOJA/OBATALA	ESU ADE WA	ENI OSHUN
127) 07/31/04 SEKANI	ESHU FUNMI L'ODUN	ELEGBA/OSHUN	ADE LETI	EFUN L'OKE
128) 02/12/05 EBONY	SHANGO DE	SHANGO/YEMOJA	OSA YEMISI	OKE SANDE
129) 06/11/05 TAMIKO	AYABA N'ILE	OBA/SHANGO	ORISAIYE	OKE L'OLA
130) 07/16/05 MONIQUE	EFUN ARO	OBATALA/OSHUN	ORISAIYE	OMI DURO
131) 04/22/06 KIKI	OBA SHOLA	SHANGO/OSHUN	ESHU ADE WA	OKANIGBE
132) 06/3/06 MONICA	SOLA KEMI	AGANJU/OSHUN	OMI LETI	OKE SANDE
133) 07/29/06 MARIO	OSHUN T'OLA	OSHUN/IBU KOLE	OKE L'OLA	ORISAIYE

187

134) 10/21/06	DEBORAH	BABA K'OLEYO	OBATALA/YEMONJA	BABA 'SHEGUN	OKUN AINA
135) 01/26/07	FOLASADE	OMI T'OLA	YEMONJA/OBATALA	ESU 'SHEGUN	OKE SANDE
136) 03/17/07	ESMERALDA	XXXXXXX	SHANGO/YEMONJA	ORISAIYE	OKE L'OLA
137) 04/21/07	XXXXXX	AFEFE LEKUN	OBATALA/OSHUN	ODU BI	OSHUN FUNMI
138) 07/14/07	OLUGBADE	OGUN DEI	OGUN/OYA	OKE SANDE	IRIN T'OLA
139) 02/23/08	TIFFANY	OBA INA	AGANJU/OBATALA	OSA YEMISI	OMI LERI
140) 07/19/08	PHILIP	OKUN TOLADE	YEMONJA/SHANGO	BABA 'SEGUN	ORISAIYE
141) 08/09/08	ANNETTA	ADE SINA	OBATALA/OSHUN	OSHUN KO LADE	OKE SANDE
142) 08/09/08	AMEENAH	SHANGO LARI	SHANGO/OSHUN	ESHU ADE WA	SHANGO DEI
143) 09/27/08	INDIRA	OMI SHEGUN	YEMONJA/ELEGBA	OKANIGBE	OSHUN ATILEWA
144) 02/12/10	JAMES	ILARI OKE	AGANJU/OYA	OBA NI L'AYE	TENU LERI
145) 05/28/10	ATHENA	ADE DOYIN	OBATALA/OYA	OKE SANDE	OSHUN KO L'ADE
146) 05/28/10	ITALA	OMI L'OOGUN	YEMONJA/ELEGBA	OKE SANDE	OSHUN MOREMI
147) 07/10/10	XXXXXXX	XXXXXXX	ELEGBA/OYA	OYA NI YI	ORISAIYE
148) 09/03/10	VICKI	OBA N'ILE	SHANGO/YEMONJA	ORISAIYE	OMI LETI
149) 09/18/10	SIMONE	OYA AKIN SHOLA	OYA/ELEGBA	OSHUN KO L'ADE	OSA YEMISI

188

150) 10/09/10	SHARON	OYA FUNMI	OYA/OBATALA	· OKE SANDE	OSHUN FUNMI
151) 01/22/11	DOROTHY	OSHUN IYA LAGBARA	OSHUN/OBATALA	OYA NI YI	OMI DURO
152) 08/04/11	FRANKLIN	OGUN JOBI	OGUN/OBA	ESHU ADE WA	ODE SHEGUN
153) 09/03/11	TINA	OYA BODE	OYA/SHANGO	ESHU ADE WA	EGUIN KOIDE
154) 11/11/11	ZYLANA	ESHU DAMIOLA	ELEGBA/OSHUN	OYA TOKUN'BO	ORISAIYE
155) 11/11/11	ONILADE	OKE L'ADE	OBATALA/OSHUN	OYA TOKUN'BO	SHANGO DE
156) 01/28/12	JUDSON	SHANGO BUNMI	SHANGO/OYA	ESHU ADE WA	ODE SHEGUN
157) 07/08/12	CHARLES	ESHU OKANTOMI	ELEGBA/OYA	ESHU ADE WA	ADE L'OKUN
158) 08/03/12	AYOTIDE	SHANGO ALA BI	SHANGO/YEMONJA	EFUN L'OKE	ORISAIYE
159) 10/20/12	AMETHYST	XXXXXXXX	OYA/ELEGBA	OYA NI YI	ORUNMIADE

189

Made in the USA
Charleston, SC
20 October 2013